"Clayton and Charie share truth and wisdom that I believe will help young Christian couples build strong relationships that will last for a lifetime."

—**JERRY FALWELL JR.**, chancellor and president,
Liberty University

"In a day when the church desperately needs its people to show the reality of the gospel to a lost world by how we love each other in our marriages, I cannot think of a better book for Christians to read and implement than this one."

—**PERRY NOBLE,** senior pastor, Newspring Church,
Anderson, South Carolina

"Clayton and Charie King have done a fantastic job of preparing young men and women for marriage by encouraging them to ask commonsense questions that reveal very important issues of character, conviction, and competence. I urge you to read this book."

—**DANIEL AKIN,** president,
Southeastern Baptist Theological Seminary
and author of *God on Sex*

"I know that God will use this book to impact thousands—my prayer is that you will allow this book to impact *you*."

—**JONATHAN FALWELL,** pastor,
[ ] Baptist Church
[Lync]hburg, Virginia

"This book [ ] [refre]shing warning signs. It enc[ ] [des]ires with biblical truth. I [ ] [es]."

—[ ] [LI]NTON, president,
[Chri]stian Counselors

"With God's direction through this powerful book, I pray you'll find t[...] answers that lead you to the one-of-a-kind love story God has written f[...] your life."

—from the foreword by **CRAIG GROESCHEL**, auth[...] founding and senior pastor of LifeChurch[...]

"This helpful book advises young adults to look past sentimental notions [...] romance to see the challenges and rewards of the reality of lifelong comm[...] ment. Clayton and Charie offer strong medicine that will lead to strong[...] families."

—**TREVIN WAX**, author
Counterfeit Gospels and *Holy Subversi*[...]

"Clayton and Charie have written a gift to the church, a book on relatic[...] ships that meets all of us wherever we are and spurs us on towards the g[...] cious Lordship of Jesus Christ."

—**MATT ORTH**, pas[...]
Broad River Community Chur[...]
Boiling Springs, North Caroli[...]

"Whether you're single or married, this book is essential reading."

—**STEVEN FURTICK**, lead pas[...]
Elevation Church, Charlotte, North Caroli[...]
author, *Sun Stand S*[...]

12 Questions
to Ask
Before You Marry

Clayton and Charie King

HARVEST HOUSE PUBLISHERS

EUGENE, OREGON

Cover by Dugan Design Group, Bloomington, Minnesota

Cover photo © Serena Siqueland / Digital Vision / Getty Images; back-cover author photo © Bob Carey

Clayton and Charie King's agent: David Van Diest from D.C. Jacobson & Associates, 3689 Carman Dr., Ste. 300, Lake Oswego, OR.

Personal stories in this book: Where individuals may be identifiable, they have granted the author and the publisher the right to use their names, stories, and/or facts of their lives in all manners, including composite or altered representations. In all other cases, names, circumstances, descriptions, and details have been changed to render individuals unidentifiable.

12 QUESTIONS TO ASK BEFORE YOU MARRY
Copyright © 2011 by Clayton and Charie King
Published by Harvest House Publishers
Eugene, Oregon 97402
www.harvesthousepublishers.com

Library of Congress Cataloging-in-Publication Data
King, Clayton, 1972-
12 questions to ask before you marry / Clayton and Charie King.
p. cm.
ISBN 978-0-7369-3777-1 (pbk.)
ISBN 978-0-7369-4195-2 (eBook)
1. Marriage—Religious aspects—Christianity. I. King, Charie, 1974- II. Title.
BV835.K545 2011
241'.6765—dc22

2011007471

Printed in the United States of America

11 12 13 14 15 16 17 18 19 / VP-SK / 10 9 8 7 6 5 4 3 2 1

A Word of Thanks from Clayton

I thank my family (Joe, Jane, and Brad) for adopting me, loving me, teaching me hard work and humility, and raising me to know and love Christ.

I am thankful for good friends like Matt, Seth, Perry, Steven, Jonathan, Brian, J.D., Bruce, Dean, Justin, Micah, Jeremy, Brad, Brent, Jordan, Johnnie, David, Tyler, Paul, Todd, Andy, and Ray for their faithfulness to Jesus and to me.

I am thankful for godly mentors like Wilkes Skinner, Jake Thornhill, Doug Murphy, and Billy Graham who have modeled what it means to follow Christ and be a servant.

I am thankful for the many preachers and authors who have shaped my life and theology.

I am thankful for the staff at Crossroads, the community at Broad River, and everyone at Newspring and Liberty for their prayers and support over the years.

Most of all I am thankful to, and for, my wife, Charie, and our boys, Jacob and Joseph. You are the joy of my life. I love you so very much.

Contents

✳

Foreword

by Craig Groeschel

Most marriages begin with dreams of happily ever after. In reality, more than half of those unions won't see that fairy-tale ending—but they will end. And of the marriages that do last, many struggle on life support for the "sake of the kids."

It doesn't have to be that way.

It's not supposed to be that way.

So what do you do when you want a marriage that soars in a world where most crash before takeoff? What do you do when you have a dream for intimacy, but most married couples you know are strangers to each other? What do you do when you desire a marriage that honors God and goes the distance?

You do something different.

Think about it. The normal path toward marriage isn't working very well, is it? Premarital sex is par for the course. Living together before marriage is seen as an acceptable decision. And many individuals plow through person after person, as if buying dozens of lottery tickets hoping for the lucky one—the one that might hold the magic ticket of marriage.

When you think about it, many people desperate for love attempt to find it by doing what married people do. They share their hearts. *I love you.* They share their bodies. *I want you.* They share their living spaces. *Let's move in together.* In other words, they pretend like they are married. When their imaginary marriage doesn't work, they break it off. Pretend marriage. Practice divorce.

Before long, rather than seeing marriage as a covenant before God, they view it as a contract to protect themselves. I'll do my part. You do yours. I'm in as far as you're in. Once the real marriage hits some inevitable bumps along the road, they naturally do what they trained to do: They bail at the nearest off-ramp and go their separate ways.

Thankfully, Clayton and Charie King have written a book with some different advice. While some claim to have all the answers, Clayton and Charie take another approach. You might say they have all the questions. The eye-opening book they've written, *12 Questions to Ask Before You Marry*, will show you that your craving for lifelong intimacy is a God-given desire. With wisdom, humor, and practical advice, they'll help you prepare for that God-honoring relationship.

Let me warn you: The questions in this book might lead you toward some different answers. In fact, I pray they do. If you are sick of dead-end relationships or lukewarm love, it's time to make some major changes. If small changes would do the trick, everyone would be making them. Minor adjustments produce marginal results. Most of us need to overhaul our thinking. To experience the kind of relationships we long for, we must, with God's help, prepare to be radically different.

It's time to ask the right questions. And with God's direction through this powerful book, I pray you'll find the answers that lead you to the one-of-a-kind love story God has written for your life.

—*Craig Groeschel*
author; founding and senior
pastor of LifeChurch.tv

Are You Paying Attention?

Everyone is going somewhere. Only a few people go there on purpose. Charie and I aren't sure who came up with this saying. But we're sure that it's true. We're also fairly certain that few people ever consider the end of their lives while they're still young. If they think about it at all, most people assume that life just happens, and you react to it as best you can.

Americans are particularly susceptible to living life on automatic pilot. We get so distracted by work and school and entertainment and relationships that we fail to realize that every single day, we are heading in a direction, toward a destination, a place at the end of our lives where we will look back with great joy or great regret.

If you're not paying attention to your life and your relationships, they will still happen. Just not the way you want them to.

If you make bad decisions and never stop to ask where they will take you, you will, one day, look back on a life filled with wasted opportunities and failures.

If you act wisely, pay attention, choose the right direction, and ask the right questions, you will look back on your life with great joy and satisfaction.

The strange thing to us is that so many people find themselves in circumstances they did not desire and, against all common sense, they wonder how they got there.

Most of us are usually able to see the disconnect in our friends and peers when this happens to them. When they freak out because of something that's gone wrong in their lives, we secretly want to scream at them, "Didn't you see this coming? Because I sure did!"

The irony is how fast we notice these bad choices in others and how slowly we notice them in ourselves.

It's the human default mechanism. We naturally look for someone or something else to blame when we wind up in a mess. And it's really hard to pay attention to our own shortcomings when there are so many to look at in other people.

Nowhere is this more pronounced than in the area of love and relationships.

Attention, Direction, Destination

Of all the rich, glorious, satisfying things God has placed in our world for our enjoyment, nothing comes close to the breathtaking joy of a great marriage that's centered around God. A loving, lifelong relationship is the apex of human experience. Trust us...you do *not* want to miss out on something this good! We know because, in His grace, God has led us into that kind of marriage. That is why we want you to pay attention—because your attention leads you to a direction, and your direction takes you to a destination. After knowing Christ, a fulfilling marriage and a loving family are the greatest goals we can aspire to in this life. If you get there, it will be because you *paid attention*, *chose a direction*, and *arrived at a destination* (thank you to Andy Stanley for teaching me this!).

Charie and I have spent quite a bit of time listening to men and women with relationship issues that resulted from not paying attention or choosing the wrong direction. Our life together as a married couple has been a round-the-clock time of working with people. Between the two of us we have five decades of doing this. We have taken engaged couples through formal marriage counseling. We have stayed up into the wee hours of the morning listening to young adults go back and forth wondering if they should stay in a relationship or walk away. We have listened on the other end of a phone call from a wife who just found out her husband had been having an adulterous affair for years.

Each of us could also testify to the wreckage and destruction we have witnessed firsthand among our friends, family members, classmates, and co-workers. Even if you're not married yet, you almost certainly know someone who tried marriage and decided it wasn't worth it. For whatever reason, they threw in the towel and called it quits.

And when a marriage is broken apart, people get hurt. Every single time.

But Charie and I want you to see that marriage is not meant to hurt you. It was planned and put together by the Grand Designer Himself to help you, bless you, make you a better person, show you how to give and receive love, and allow you to share deep, abiding joy with one other person for life.

To put it bluntly, failed relationships are now the norm. Healthy, lasting marriages are now the exception. This is simply unacceptable, and we are *not* okay with it. Neither should you be. Marriage is too good to miss or mess up! And we believe that God believes in you. He also believes in your mate, your kids, your family, and your future. And He is a good God who wants good things for you.

Remember, everyone will wind up somewhere. In a word, at their destiny. Few people get there on purpose. But you can. A healthy, godly, fulfilling marriage is a perfect example of this simple truth. Start working toward that goal *right now*. And you start by doing the one thing Mom and Dad and your teachers always told you to do.

Pay attention.

What Has Your Attention?

We're all paying attention to lots of things. If you're like us, probably too many things. Here is a short list of the things that occupy most of our mental space:

- *Our phones*: iPhones, Blackberrys, Blueberrys, Droids
- *Our messages*: texts, tweets, Facebook, e-mails, voice mails

- *Our jobs*: getting there on time, working with excellence, praying our employer doesn't downsize

- *Our education*: studying for exams, doing research for papers, working on projects, trying to graduate

- *Our debts*: student loans, credit cards, mortgages, car payments

- *Our health*: trying to eat right, cutting down on calories, doing some exercise, getting to the gym, going to bed earlier, cutting back on caffeine

- *Our entertainment*: cable TV, iPads, iPods, iTunes, Kindle and Nook and e-readers, laptops, NetFlix, Xboxes

- *Our social life*: hanging with friends, going out to eat, concerts and movies, attending parties and get-togethers, taking fun trips to do fun stuff

You can relate to some of these, right? Because the truth is we are all paying attention to *something*. But are we paying attention to the *right things*?

We begin paying attention to the opposite sex at the stage of puberty, usually around middle school.

We start "dating." We get a boyfriend or a girlfriend. We base all our decisions on how we feel, so when our feelings change (and they do change a lot with teenagers), we just break up. We find someone new. Date them until we don't feel the attraction anymore, or until someone better comes along. Then we break up again. And repeat. What begins as a relationship experience in middle school becomes a habit in high school. That high-school bad habit follows us into college and becomes a lifestyle of temporary togetherness. Once college comes to an end, we've practiced a destructive and unhealthy form of relationships for eight or ten years…and we wonder why on earth we can't make love stick. The truth is, we are creatures of habit, and the habits we formed in adolescence follow us into adulthood.

We get divorce practice through the repeated cycle of dating and breaking up. We learn bad habits by making bad choices and then bailing out before real consequences set in. Or so we think!

The real world is designed in such a way that all decisions have consequences. Some sooner, some later. Some good, some bad. Eventually, we pay the price or reap the benefits for the direction we choose in our relationships. And that consequence for millions of adult Americans is depression, anxiety, and bitterness, all resulting from an unhealthy marriage. For Charie and me, by God's grace, the benefits are love, joy, trust, peace, happiness, and satisfaction.

It really makes you wonder about a simple question. Is anybody paying attention?

THAT'S A GOOD QUESTION...

If you're paying attention to your life and your future at all, you need to be asking questions like these.

- Why do so few people stay married anymore?

- Why are antidepressants one of the most commonly prescribed medications in America now?

- Why are sexually active teenagers more likely to perform poorly in school?

- Why are students who come from divorced families more susceptible to emotional problems, becoming gang members, depression, and alcohol abuse?

- Is there a correlation between the breakdown of the American family and lower test scores for American students—lower than any time in the past 50 years?

- Why do 40 percent of U.S. citizens say that the idea of a traditional marriage with one man and one woman for life is out-of-date and irrelevant?

- Why do a growing percentage of American teenagers engage in ritualistic self-mutilation, a practice called "cutting," which they say helps them release their inner pain?

- Why are more Americans delaying marriage till their late twenties and early thirties—after they have prioritized their careers?

- Why are more married couples having kids later in their marriages, or opting not to have children at all?

- Why do psychologists say that the divorce of parents is harder on children emotionally than the death of one of those parents?

Too Good to Miss

Marriage is the ultimate joy in all of life next to knowing Christ. It was God's idea from the very beginning of time. It's the oldest social institution on earth and the basic foundation of all societies and cultures. Through marriage we are able to bring new life into being with our children, renew hope for the human race with every new birth, learn how to serve another human being for half a century (or more), become one mind and one flesh with our mate, and care for another person with kindness and humility until death.

Consequently, we believe marriage is a big deal. Maybe the biggest deal in the whole world. It was God's idea. And marriage is so sacred that God uses it as a picture of His relationship with His own people, the church. He calls the church "the bride of Christ." That alone should grab our attention.

Charie and I want to see the trend reversed—the trend of destructive, unhealthy relationships being the norm. That is why we wrote this book.

And we want you to beat the odds. We want you to pay attention and choose the right direction. If we should meet you some day, we want to be able to celebrate with you…that you have a good marriage that honors God and shows the world a picture of His love for humanity. We don't want you to miss out on something this awesome…

- a strong marriage built on a firm foundation
- a marriage that can stand the tests and traumas that life will most certainly throw at you
- a marriage that is impervious to the drama that dominates our sick culture
- a marriage predicated on serving your spouse instead of being served by your spouse
- a marriage that gets better as it gets older
- a marriage that your children and grandkids will want to model and copy
- a marriage you can be proud, not ashamed, of
- a marriage where each of you can be who God made you to be
- a marriage where you lay down your rights and pick up your responsibilities with joy
- a marriage that pursues holiness instead of happiness… and gains both
- a marriage that is affair-proof and divorce-proof
- a marriage that produces godly, humble, healthy, children prepared for life
- a marriage that handles adversity well and stands firm in the storms of life
- a marriage that fulfills both individuals emotionally, spiritually, and sexually
- a marriage that honors God by reflecting the gospel—the sacrifice of Jesus and your new life in Him
- a marriage that is a living example of God's unconditional love for the world

If you want a relationship like that, you'll need to begin paying attention now. Forget any silly notion that attraction alone will do the trick. The Beatles were wrong. Love is *not* all you need. Take stock of your own habits. Your own character. The way you handle conflict. Your realistic and unrealistic expectations for a mate. Start paying attention to the right things.

Get Married on Purpose

Great marriages don't fall from the sky. They happen on purpose, deliberately, as a result of hard work, both before and during the relationship. But it won't seem like work at all once you experience the deep, abiding joy of being connected to a person at the heart-and-soul level and knowing that you are there for each other, no matter what, 'til death do you part.

Charie and I believe there are 12 questions you need to ask (and answer) before you walk the aisle on your wedding day. By addressing these questions and the issues they bring to the surface *before* marriage, you will uncover things you would have eventually seen *after* marriage...but by dealing with them now, you disarm the bomb before it goes off.

By waking up, paying attention, and asking questions now, you get some answers. And you end up with these benefits.

- You get honest with yourself about your own issues, sins, disappointments, and expectations.

- You see your own bad habits and foolish choices and are able to make some important course corrections.

- You can be honest about your own level of maturity...or immaturity.

- You see how your previous relationships created your emotional responses to stress, adversity, and disappointment.

- You get honest about how you've handled money in the past, how much debt you have, and how money affects marriages.

- You own up to any sexual indiscretions from your past, and repent and receive forgiveness from God so you can move on without guilt and condemnation.

- You take inventory of your emotional habits: how you process anger, deal with stress, handle adversity, and deal with conflict.

- You realize whether or not you're ready for marriage and, if not, what it will take for you to get ready.

God in His grace woke up Charie and me as teenagers. We began paying attention. We put Christ first. We practiced biblical purity. We listened to our parents and our pastors. We set high standards and worked on our relationship with the Lord. Years later, He brought us together, and today we love being together as a couple. We are best friends and lovers, and we have no secrets. We are living a dream come true.

Blindsided

There is a humorous story that perfectly illustrates what could happen to you if you're not paying attention, and unfortunately it happened to me—Clayton—in middle school.

Do you remember what that time was like? Do you remember how you looked? Somewhere in your mom's house there are pictures of you in seventh grade with a hairstyle that could make a statue laugh and braces that look like satellite dishes on your teeth. This was the age where you started wearing deodorant. You started shaving. Your body was outgrowing your coordination. And you decided that the opposite sex was no longer weird.

All of these factors added to the already embarrassing stage of life known as "middle school." I can still remember much of it like it was yesterday. Especially the event that would mark me for life, leave me in shambles, and turn me into an emotional wreck for years.

I was in the eighth grade. The previous 13 years of my life had been pretty good. I'd been adopted by an awesome Christian family when I was a few weeks old. My mom and dad loved me unconditionally and modeled a good marriage for me. But I was big. My grandma said I was "husky." I was always bigger and stronger than all of my friends, but I was still a chunky kid.

But the summer between seventh and eighth grade was magical. Perhaps it was a convergence of hormonal transition and testosterone, but I lost 30 pounds and grew four inches in three months. I left school that May as a pudgy doughboy. I returned in September as a muscled young man. And people noticed. The guys suddenly respected me. Coaches kept commenting on how big and coordinated I'd become. But most importantly, the girls began to look my way. One in particular. Mandy. (Thanks, Charie, for letting me tell about this!)

I'd had a crush on her from the first time our eyes met but she had never given me a second glance until I showed up for eighth grade looking like I'd been on HydroxyCut, a well-known "diet pill," all summer. She and I began "dating," as we called it, though we never actually went on dates. But that's beside the point.

I also had my best year in basketball and was named defensive player of the year. My PE coach coached varsity baseball as well, and he told me to try out for it in the spring because he thought I was good enough to make the team. I was too nervous and didn't want to get cut, so I declined. But after just two games, he moved me from JV to varsity and told me I would start my first game at first base, batting third in the lineup!

Word spread fast around school. High-schoolers told me they were coming to see me play. But the one person I most cared about impressing was Mandy.

When I invited Mandy to watch me play varsity, her eyes lit up. She assured me she would be there "to watch my man show everybody what he can do." (Yes, those were her exact words. I remember.)

We were warming up when I saw Mandy come to the field. My stomach was in knots. This was the single most important moment of my existence. I knew I had one shot. I had to make sure I didn't do something stupid.

We took the field, and the other team was at bat. I was playing first base. My first varsity game. Lots of pressure. My girlfriend watching. And all I could do was imagine what I would do if the ball was hit to me. I knew how I would react, how I would move. And as I was daydreaming…

I heard a sound. It was like a tree breaking or a limb snapping. It definitely sounded like wood hitting something…or something hitting wood.

Then I saw something. It was coming right at me. It was moving so fast I really didn't know what to make of it. It was white and blurry, and it seemed to be spherical.

It was all starting to come together…the cracking sound of wood hitting an object…a small white circular object moving toward me at a rapid velocity…I almost had it figured out when—

WHACK.

I thought someone had shot me right between the eyes. My first idea was that I'd been assassinated, until I realized no one would want to assassinate me. Then everything went black, but not before I felt myself falling backward toward the ground. Then I saw Julie Andrews dancing on the top of a mountain in Austria, singing, "The hills are alive with the sound of music."

When I came to, my coach was helping me stand up. I felt like I'd been asleep for a long time, I heard chatter from the players and the fans. I looked around, a bit shakily, and everyone was staring at me, laughing. My coach held up the round white object and said, "Clayton, this is a baseball. And in the game of baseball, the most important thing is to always pay attention."

Then it all came together. While I was lost in imagination, dreaming of what it would be like for the ball to get hit toward me, the pitcher had thrown the first pitch and the batter, a left-hander, had hit a line drive right at my head. It had nailed me right between the eyes and knocked me out cold.

I walked around for three days with an imprint of the baseball's stitching on my forehead. I fell like Goliath, but was resurrected like Lazarus.

In short, I was blindsided. I never saw it coming.

That's my baseball story. But that doesn't have to be your marriage story.

Think about it. If you were to get married today, at your maturity level, with your habits, and treat your marriage like you have treated all your other dating relationships, would it be a healthy, holy marriage?

God wants you to experience His very best for you, so He has already given you His best gift in Jesus Christ. Next to His Son, the greatest gift God will ever give you will be the person you marry. What you do with that person and that relationship is up to you. You can choose a path that will lead you to a divorce-proof marriage filled with joy and triumphs and the presence of God. You can begin to make small investments now that will pay big dividends later—investments in your maturity, your character, your personal relationship with God, your attitude toward money, your habits, and your behavior patterns. You don't have to get hit between the eyes and knocked out cold.

As you travel with us, stay aware of a few things. These will make your journey more enjoyable and more helpful to you.

1. We wrote every single word in this book to help you and serve you by encouraging you to ask important questions before you get married. We love you and only want to help you, by God's grace.

2. A failed relationship or a divorce is not a death sentence. God gives second chances, and you can still have the marriage you've always dreamed of.

3. We believe that God wants the absolute best for you. Marriage should be the ultimate joy, and hard work will get you there.

You might as well start now, right? So begin with the end in mind. Ask the tough questions. Charie and I wrote this book to help you chart a course to a lifelong love that honors God and leaves a legacy long after you're gone.

Oh yes…if you've read this far, I think it's safe to officially say that you are paying attention. Congratulations! Now that we have your attention, let's move on to the next question.

Chapter 1

Are You Willing to Grow Up?

Then we will no longer be infants, tossed back and forth…
Instead, speaking the truth in love, we will in all things
grow up into him who is the Head, that is, Christ.
EPHESIANS 4:14-15

Here is the best advice on marriage and relationships I have ever heard in my life. Partially because it is simple, blunt, and easy to remember. Mostly because it is absolutely true. Are you ready? *Grow up.*

Rick Warren, the well-known author and pastor from California, said that after 30 years of marriage and relationship counseling sessions, he could sum up nearly all of what needs to be said to both men and women in those two words—*grow up*. I agree.

That is why Charie and I chose to put this chapter near the beginning. Right off the bat, straight out of the gate, you need to know that just about every other problem or challenge or struggle that arises in your marriage will only be a secondary issue. The primary issue will be your level of maturity. Because that maturity, above all other things, will determine whether or not you work together as a team to solve problems or whether you act like children, puffing and pouting and pontificating under pressure, and eventually quitting the relationship.

The bottom line is simple. Marriage is for grown-ups. It is too difficult and requires too much effort, patience, and self-control for people with the maturity level of children. And keep this point in mind: Maturity is not about your age. It is about your acceptance of responsibility.

Acting Like a Kid

There is something epic, right, and good about watching a mom or a dad lay down the law with their five-year-old in the grocery store. I've always been impressed with parents who are firm with their kids and aren't swayed by their emotional outbursts and toddler tirades. So many kids rule and reign over their parents, ignoring their warnings, flopping about on the floor like a smallmouth bass out of water. So when a mom or dad actually follows through on a threat by stopping their child from behaving badly, popping them on the bottom, or grabbing them by the hand and taking them outside to the car or the parking lot, I just want to shout with joy. It's beautiful to watch a mom or a dad accept the responsibility of being the parent. They're acting like grown-ups. And one day their children will also act like grown-ups because their responsible parents taught them how to be responsible for their actions from their earliest years.

I saw something along these lines unfold one day in the post office that left an indelible mark on me. It involved a mom and her son. And it's the perfect illustration of what happens when adults refuse to grow up, to mature, before they tie the knot.

I was behind them in line observing the interaction between mommy and son. This kid was...I really don't know how to describe him. Awful? Disrespectful? Obnoxious? None of these do him justice. Put plainly, the kid was out of control. Yelling, jumping, pulling envelopes off the shelves. His mom was pitiful. Threatening him. Screaming at him. Rolling her eyes and snapping her fingers. It was a just a big display of futility. The kid knew his mom wasn't going to follow through with any of her threats. They had played this game before. He knew he could act however he wanted and get away with it.

Everyone there was embarrassed. The clerks looked frazzled. But all of the grown-ups in the room knew it was not the five-year-old who was to blame. It was his mother. Even though she had accumulated enough years to be considered a grown-up, she was, in a sense, as immature as her son.

Then everything changed. The boy was running in and out of the large, heavy swinging doors that led to the parking lot. These were thick glass doors with steel frames. Every time he would run through them, he would push them open really hard, and try to jump back through them before they would close. And they would bang closed.

As the tiny tyrant was playing his game while his mother screamed more threats at him, an older woman with both hands full of boxes opened the other swinging door. And right as that door began to swing backward, the kid was jumping through, playing his game. He never saw the door the woman had let go.

The timing was perfect. The physics were just right. The door caught the boy at just the right angle and at full velocity as he came full-speed toward it. The kid was maybe 40 pounds, the door was at least 150 pounds, and he went airborne.

It sounded and looked way worse than it actually was. He was scared out of his mind. There was no blood, no real injury. But it was as if the cosmic forces of justice and discipline decided to step in and deal with a young boy whose mother was not willing to. All of us in the post office froze until we realized he was okay. And as he shrieked and cried and screamed bloody murder, we tried our best not roll on the floor laughing.

For some of you, sadly, this will be your marriage story. Playing games, having fun, acting like a child, when—BOOM! Out of nowhere you will get sideswiped and knocked on your back, and wonder what in the world happened.

Acting Your Age

People who are willing to grow up are developing the wisdom and foresight to look ahead and predict the outcomes of the decisions they make. If they don't like what they see in their future, they make changes. They redirect their spending. They pick new friends. They begin reading books and turn off the TV and computer. They put away their cell phones when they need time to think. They watch what they eat. They adjust how they handle relationships.

Fools are not willing to grow up. They like being able to have fun and do what they want. They can run around and scream and yell and pull stuff off the shelves, so to speak. And they can play silly little games with other people's hearts and emotions. They can sleep around, fool around, and break up with people at will. But just like the rowdy kid in the post office, if they refuse to grow up, hoping a great marriage will automatically come along someday, they will get blindsided by a force bigger and stronger than them. The kid never saw the door coming. Millions of people each year never see the divorce, the affair, or the meltdown coming.

Mature adults see trouble in the future as a result of their current decisions, and they change. Immature kids don't.

This is why God gave us parents. Whether yours were good or bad, the job of parents is to guide and protect their children, preparing them to be mature adults in the real world one day. All good parents have, at one time or another, told their child to "act your age." The assumption is that if a child is eight years old, they aren't allowed to roll around on the floor in the middle of Wal-Mart like a two-year-old who doesn't get the toy they want. There is an expectation that is not only natural but also normal. There needs to be level of maturity that is equivalent to the number of years a person has been alive.

So before you tie the knot, it is paramount that you deal with this issue as quickly as possible. Again, every single issue and problem and misunderstanding you face in your future as a married man or woman will be framed by your maturity level. If you have never really grown up emotionally, you will find yourself in the midst of a disagreement over something as insignificant as whose family you will visit over the Christmas holidays, and before you know it, it has blown up, and so have you, into an all-out fight. And you (or maybe both of you) are dredging up things from years past, making accusations that are irrelevant to the decision about Christmas plans, and raising your voices to the decibel level of a Metallica concert...all because you did not get your way in the discussion.

Be honest. Do you ever do this? Internally or externally? If you've never really asked yourself this question, you should do it right now.

And answer truthfully. There is nobody to judge you or make you feel bad. I'm not here watching you—I wrote these words long before you picked up our book. So what do you have to gain by being dishonest about your maturity level? Just own up to it and tell the truth. It's the first step in preparing yourself to be the kind of woman or man who is ready for the lifelong commitment of marriage.

Read the Signs

On the next couple of pages, you'll find a basic list of words, attitudes, behaviors, actions, and reactions to serve as a grid...a grid by which you can judge your own level of emotional, spiritual, social, and financial maturity. Look at them as you would look at road signs.

The department of motor vehicles in your state will not issue you a driver's license until you can prove to them (on a test, administered in a crowded building by less-than-happy DMV employees, usually) that you not only know how to read all road signs, but that you can also interpret what they mean. The DMV wants to know that you are competent enough to obey posted signs—signs that indicate laws that were established for our protection.

God has established laws in the universe He created. His laws are for our benefit and blessing, to protect us and keep us from harming others and ourselves. He has given us signs that He cares for us by establishing laws governing our behavior. He's given us the Bible, the church, pastors and teachers and leaders, our parents, coaches, and the experience of older people to warn us. If we ignore the signs, we pay the price, just as ignoring road signs could cost us a speeding ticket or a head-on collision. It could cost us a fine, our privilege of driving, or even our life. So it's much better to read the signs and obey them. Or as one observer of life has pointedly reminded all of us, "You better check yourself before you wreck yourself."

As you consider your maturity level, do not be discouraged if you realize that you do indeed need to grow up in one or more areas. Rather, be motivated to change, make course corrections, get help, seek a mentor, read some books, see a counselor, change jobs. If you merely feel bad over being immature, you've missed the point. Think of these words as shining a light into your life that will illuminate you to yourself.

You may need to grow up if…

You are over 30 years old and still live with your parents. With the exceptions of caring for aging or sick family members or the sudden loss of a job, by your thirties, unless there is a physical or mental limitation, you should be self-sufficient enough to leave the nest. Who really wants to marry someone who still lives in their parents' basement at age 34?

You have never had a job of any kind for more than six months. If you have never worked, you need a job. Any job will do. Just start somewhere. You need the experience. If you've had numerous jobs over the years and none of them have lasted very long, it may be a sign that you are lazy or easily bored, or have a problem being told what to do by a boss.

You are unable to pay your basic bills each month. Without assistance from family members or friends, you simply could not make it financially. This includes car insurance, rent, groceries, power bill, and basic medical expenses. If you can't pay your basic bills, you will cause a train wreck by getting married to someone.

As a general rule, you lack self-control in your life. Whether it's your spending habits, how much you eat, the amount of time you spend watching TV, or your constant obsession with being online (checking e-mail, Facebook, Twitter, or YouTube), these are signs of immaturity, and are a crucial red flag that points to an inability to control your desires.

Your relationships look more like a roller coaster than a marathon. You are unable to develop long-term relationships with the opposite sex. You've never learned how to push through problems, boredom, or conflict, and your default mechanism is to break it off and start a new one. Your past is filled with failure in the area of commitment.

You always play the victim. You're always secretly trying to uncover a conspiracy by your peers to exclude you from social outings, parties, get-togethers, or group dates. It's immature to think that the cosmic forces of nature and love have combined their powers to hurt *you*. None of us are that important in the grand scheme of things.

You tend to speak negatively of other people. Whether in one-on-one conversations or in large groups, your habit is to bash or attack someone who is not present to defend themselves. Immature people say things about people behind their back (or online) that they would never dream of saying to their face. This can ruin a marriage in a hurry, because it reveals deep insecurities.

You are plagued by jealousy. Little children get upset on the playground when they see their best friend playing with or talking to another child. Grown-ups get past this stage…at least they should. Are you consistently jealous of other people's possessions, salaries, houses, cars, friends, physical appearance, or family? Can you celebrate the blessings of God in others' lives? Or does God's goodness to others stir up envy inside your heart toward them?

You have trouble finishing. My two sons are notorious for starting little projects around the house, getting bored, and then abandoning them for us to clean up. They don't know how to finish things yet because they're not even ten years old. If you are known for beginning things all gung-ho with great passion, but you consistently fizzle out and never see it through, this is a relationship killer. Marriage is not something you can start, then walk away from, without serious emotional damage. Grown-ups finish what they start.

You are crippled by debt. If you are single and want to get married, the most practical area of your life to examine is your finances. This is the issue most couples fight about most often. If you owe tens of thousands of dollars on credit cards, student loans, your car, and so on, then your problem is not your debt. It's immaturity. You haven't yet learned how to live within your means.

You can't say *no*. Marriage by nature requires you to say "no" to thousands of other opportunities (and possible mates) so that you can say "yes" to one person for a lifetime. If you are the guy or the girl who is always taking care of others, bailing your friends out, staying up 'til 2 a.m. on the phone trying to talk them out of another crisis, then you will have a rude awakening once your mate expects you to give them your undivided attention and affection.

You fall in love too fast. How many times have you told someone that you were "in love" with them since you turned 18? This may be an indication that you need to mature emotionally. Falling in love after every first date shows you haven't really moved very far toward emotional maturity. It also guarantees you will get hurt as often as you fall in love, leaving your heart wounded for years to come.

Your relationships are too physical. If you have a track record of messing around and messing up with just about everyone you've ever liked or dated, this is bad news. When you start out basing a relationship on making out, kissing, or fooling around physically, you teach yourself to ignore the other person, their feelings, and the self-control that is essential in a godly marriage. Adults draw the line and stand back. Children run ahead without caution and suffer for it.

You have a problem with authority. Pay attention to this one, because marriage is about submitting completely, heart and soul, to someone else. Children hate being told what to do, regardless of their inability to be responsible for themselves. Are you like that? Do you tend to rebel against all forms of authority in your life? Do you balk at being told what to do by the government, the IRS, even a traffic policeman? Grown-ups understand that submission to authority is in their best interest, and they are willing to submit to God first and then to one another. Immature kids rebel.

DO I NEED TO GROW UP?

I vividly remember the moment in my life when I started to ask that question.

I'd been dating a girl off and on for about four years. We were both in college, in our early twenties, and hopelessly "in love" with each other. There were only a few minor problems.

1. Neither one of us could ever feel any sense of peace from God that we should get married.

2. We came from totally different backgrounds.

3. Our families were as different as night and day.

4. Her parents begged her to break up with me (a real bummer for a dating relationship).

5. We had fairly consistent arguments about meaningless things where one or both of us would end up in tears. (As I said, a few *minor* problems.)

It was during one of our arguments about something totally insignificant that I had a sort of "out-of-body" experience. It was as if I was looking at myself from above, and what I saw scared me because it was really happening.

I was sitting on the floor, frustrated and angry and confused. I was crying like a baby. She was lying on the floor, balled up in the fetal position, weeping and wailing and telling me how I never listened. It occurred to me that this scene looked like an episode of *The Jerry Springer Show*. We were both acting like little children.

Then and there the reality set in. We were not ready for marriage. We couldn't even have a healthy dating relationship. We were totally wrong for each other.

I broke it off and never looked back. My problem was immaturity. I needed to grow up.

✳

In the remainder of the book Charie and I will explore these ideas and encourage you to continue asking yourself difficult questions as you prepare yourself to become the kind of woman or man that is ready for the lifelong commitment of marriage. You may want to come back to the list in this chapter and glance at it as you read, asking yourself if your biggest issue is your maturity level.

Remember, everything you face in marriage can be dealt with and handled correctly if you and your spouse have the maturity to work together as a team, by God's grace, to tackle any problem that comes your way.

In what areas of your life do you need to grow up?

Chapter 2

Are You "Equally Yoked"?

*Do not be yoked together with unbelievers. For what
do righteousness and wickedness have in common? Or
what fellowship can light have with darkness? What
harmony is there between Christ and Belial? What
does a believer have in common with an unbeliever?*

2 Corinthians 6: 14-15

When we incorporated our Christian enterprise as a nonprofit
organization back in the mid-1990s, I had a friend who was
an attorney, and he did all the paperwork and IRS filings for
free. He also gave me some free advice. He said, "Never go into partnership with a friend in business. It will ruin the friendship. Partnerships never last in business." I thought he was crazy, and wrong. I pretty
much ignored the advice and plowed ahead with my plans to work
with a friend in the nonprofit.

My attorney, as it turns out, was right. A short time after we began
the organization, the friendship ended. However, the attorney had seen
this coming (he had also seen my obstinacy) so he had set up the nonprofit with me as president...just in case anything like this happened.
His foresight was a blessing.

What he saw was based on experience. He knew that when people
are working together for a common purpose and money is exchang-
ing hands, the business itself will tie partners together. It creates a bond

that forces "partners" to work together. And in business, partnerships very seldom last.

My friend and I were tied together. Another way to say it is that we were "yoked" together. Yet we had very different ideas about what the organization was supposed to look like. We disagreed on how it should be run. We argued over who was the boss and who made big decisions. Our visions did not match up. Our ideas were not aligned. We were unequally yoked. And it wasn't long before one of us had to go.

The same is true with marriage. If you marry the wrong person, then you will have "yoked up" with someone you had no business being tied to.

But what does "yoke" really mean?

Marriage and Oxen

Two thousand years ago in ancient Palestine, much of the population lived in rural areas. While cities like Rome, Athens, and Jerusalem boasted large populations, much of what Jesus said in the Gospels was geared toward common, blue-collar folks. Many of them were farmers. And even those who did not work on the land were still familiar with agricultural analogies used by Jesus and Paul, because the entire culture revolved around farms where food was grown that fed the population.

Paul borrows from such agricultural imagery here as he writes his letter to his Christian brothers and sisters in the church that existed in the Greek city of Corinth. Two thousand years later, the wisdom is still intact, and the point remains the same.

It's foolish for a Christian to marry an unbeliever.

The symbolism Paul used was immediately grasped by everyone in the Corinthian church. A yoke was a long, heavy piece of wood. It fit across the back of the necks of two farm animals (usually oxen or donkeys), and its purpose was to tie those two animals together for the purpose of plowing a field, drawing a cart, and so on. The yoke could not be broken, and once it was locked in place the animals were inescapably connected to one another. Where one went, the other went. They had no more ability to make decisions on their own. Ideally, every movement by one animal was mirrored by the other. They became like Siamese twins, as it were—mirror images of each other.

The yoke actually made the two animals one animal.

They lost all autonomy and individual freedom once the yoke was in place.

Do you see the analogy come into focus now? Marriage is like a yoke. And Paul is warning us not to be yoked up with someone who does not follow the same God we follow. Just as it's impossible for two animals yoked together to go in two different directions, it's impossible for a Christian and a non-Christian, heading in two different directions, to be yoked in marriage and not suffer greatly.

This was a major issue in the church in the city of Corinth. The entire economic system there revolved around two industries: trade and prostitution. The city had been built around the ports that existed on its shores. These ports allowed ships from all over the Mediterranean and Aegean to dock in Corinth, load and unload their cargo, trade and do business. And it was a very busy port because of its strategic location. It was constantly abuzz with activity.

As history has proven, there is one profession that almost always springs up anywhere there are ships and ports and sailors—prostitution. When the sailors would disembark from their ships in Corinth, there would be a flock of prostitutes waiting for them, dressed to kill, selling their services. The shipping and trade industry had given birth to this "cottage" industry, and it in turn had made many businessmen very rich. As long as there was a steady stream of sailors getting off boats in Corinth, the money kept flowing to the pimps who made their wealth from their girls.

Thus, the city was notorious for its sexual perversion. It was said that the temple to the goddess Diana in Corinth boasted a thousand temple prostitutes (though there is no definitive evidence to this effect). Further, a sex cult pervaded the Corinthian culture. When I visited the city in 2003, I saw dozens of archaeological features and artifacts from that time period that glorified certain body parts and sexual activities that Corinth had become famous for. It was like an ancient Las Vegas or red-light district in Amsterdam.

Now imagine with me what it was like when the gospel of Jesus Christ first landed in the shipyards of Corinth. As people began to convert to faith in Christ, the only thing they had ever known was sexual license and perversion in their relationships. Everything was allowed. Nothing was off-limits. Multiple partners and orgies and incestuous relationships were the everyday norm.

Then folks began to hear the gospel. They began believing it. They were converted from their sin to faith in Christ. They became a part of the community of Christ. They began meeting in homes and sharing meals together and listening to the stories of the life of Jesus. And Paul knew that for every Corinthian convert, it was going to be a struggle to live out a new life of chastity and purity instead of license and perversion. They would be living out this new morality in perhaps the most sexually perverse city in the Roman Empire.

So it is here, in the context of Paul's attempt to protect and instruct young Christians who are just beginning to follow the teachings of Jesus, that he admonishes them to avoid being unequally yoked with, or tied to, non-Christians.

What's the Big Deal?

Right here in 2 Corinthians, as plain as day, God tells us we must not be unequally yoked with unbelievers. The context of this command is marriage. You don't have to be a Bible scholar to understand that. Just read the entire chapter and you get the point. Yet people still want to argue that this does not apply to them or that they will be the exception to this rule.

Charie and I have had hundreds of conversations over the years with single people asking why this is such a big deal. They just cannot understand why God would forbid them to love, date, and marry someone based solely on their religion or their faith. It seems judgmental, in their opinion, to say that they cannot be in a relationship with someone who is not a Christian. After all, who are they to say that they are better than anyone else just because they are a Christian?

It just doesn't make sense to many believers in Jesus Christ that God Himself forbids His own children from marrying people who do not know Jesus as their Lord and Savior. None of us like being told what we can and cannot do. We particularly can't stand being told who we can and cannot fall in love with. If there is one area of life we want to have complete freedom and autonomy in, it is the area of love and relationships. How dare God stick His nose in our business?

TRYING TO BEAT GOD'S SYSTEM

After I preached from 2 Corinthians 6 at a Christian university in Kentucky, a young woman challenged me on my logic. She approached me in utter defiance.

"I really don't know who you think you are telling me who I can and cannot date and marry. It is none of your business who I fall in love with or spend the rest of my life with," she said. "What's the big deal, anyway?"

I responded with a simple question. "Well, is it any of God's business who you fall in love with and marry?"

She was momentarily taken aback by my question. "Well, God gives us free will, and we get to choose for ourselves who we love and who we marry and who we spend our lives with."

"Yes," I said, "That is indeed true. And along with that freedom to choose, God also gives us the consequences of our choices, which will serve to remind us that He was right and we were wrong and we were foolish to think that His rules did not apply to us—as if we were going to be the first ones to figure out a way to beat His system."

Her face was flushed and she was visibly upset. So I asked her the question that revealed her real issue. "So tell me, are you dating a guy who is not a Christian?"

Of course she was! She was convicted and wanted to defend herself to me. But I was not the one speaking to her. It was the Holy Spirit.

She was dating an unbeliever. And not coincidentally, she was having sex with an unbeliever. She wanted to marry this unbeliever. In other words, she was tied to, yoked with, an unbeliever. She was in love with her boyfriend, and she didn't want to hear anything from me or from God about how this was a bad idea or how it would never work out or how in the future she would regret it or how the marriage would eventually pull her away from her faith in Jesus.

I really wish she had listened. I often wonder what happened to her and that relationship. But you don't have to wonder…diving into the darkness of a relationship that is doomed to failure or difficulty. Just listen to God and do what He says. You will be better off.

The Objections

You should not only ask yourself the big question—"Is this person a Christian?"—before you tie the knot. You should go further by looking at every single excuse you could come up with for falling in love with and marrying an unbeliever. We have done the hard work for you by compiling these nine objections here. (You're welcome!)

1. If God didn't want me to marry this person, then why did He let me fall in love with them? The assumption here is that just because you are in love with another person, it is automatically a sign that God intended for the two of you to get married. Wow…if only it were this easy to find a mate! Let's tease this out a bit.

According to this notion, when you fall in love with someone, you take that as a sign from God that you are supposed to spend your life with the person you love. All right. But what about all the different people you have ever been in love with? Were you supposed to marry them too? I was in love with five different girls in sixth grade. All in the same day. Which one was I supposed to marry? How many boyfriends have you had? How do you know that your current one is "the one"… and not the last boy you dated? If you love your current girlfriend, should you marry her right now just because you love her? What if you break up? Does that mean you missed God's will by not marrying her when you were in love with her? You know as well as we do that you are fickle and your feelings change. You could play this game all day long and it would drive you crazy.

The bottom line is, we all fall in love all the time. And we fall out of love as quickly as we fall into it because the "love" we fall into is a cultural condition that's been created and romanticized by movies and music and sitcoms. And it doesn't last. True love in a biblical sense is lifelong service and commitment to a person regardless of current emotional fluctuation (read that sentence again).

Just because you "fall in love" with someone doesn't mean God intended for you to be married. You can fall in love with the wrong person. It happens all the time. Married men fall in love with co-workers and leave their wives for their lovers. Was that God's will? Did God make them fall in love? You can fall in love with someone who is totally wrong for you. If you spend enough time with an unbeliever, you could fall for them. Stop using this flawed logic to justify your sin.

2. I know they're not a Christian, but I am going to be a witness to them. At least you are thinking spiritually when you use this objection to God's mandate to not be tied to an unbeliever romantically. Nonetheless, it doesn't work.

If you sincerely want to be a witness to the person you are dating and that is your ultimate goal, then why are you dating them? Just break off the romantic part of the relationship and focus on being their friend. Cut out all hugging and kissing and silly romantic talk. Then stick to building a friendship over the course of time that will allow you to model what a Christian is for them. Share the gospel with them and ask them if they want to repent of their sin and follow Christ.

Yet we never do this. We are not willing to cut off the emotional, romantic element of the relationship for the sake of the gospel because our real reason for being in the relationship is not to be a witness to them—it's because we like them, maybe even love them, and we want to be with them. But if they are not a disciple of the Lord Jesus Christ, we know in our gut it won't work out. So we need a way to convince ourselves that it's okay to stay with them. What better way to justify staying in a relationship with a non-Christian than to tell yourself you are going to lead them to Christ?

We could call this "missionary dating," I suppose. But how do you know that your motive for being with them is pure and not selfish? And if they do decide to become a Christian at some point, how do you know it was an authentic conversion and not just a way for them to keep you around and make sure you do what they want you to do? People fake all kinds of stuff to keep a boyfriend or a girlfriend. People will fake salvation if they think it's the only way to keep the relationship just like Christians will pretend to be concerned about being a witness to their lost boyfriend or girlfriend to justify a relationship that God forbids.

And you don't want to marry someone who told you they "got saved" while you were dating, and then a year into the marriage you find out they were faking it for your sake. Then you really have a problem.

3. I asked God to take away my feelings for them, and He hasn't, so it must be His will that we get married. Think about it: Just because you have a feeling or a desire for something and God doesn't take it away, does that mean He gave you that desire and you should go for it? Okay—you like someone. You ask God to take away your feelings for them if He doesn't want you to date them or marry them. He *doesn't* take away the feelings. Then that's a green light straight from Him?

This is deadly and illogical, and it doesn't work in any other area of life.

Does God take away all evil desires because we ask Him to, or does He give us wisdom and self-discipline to choose to say no to those desires?

If right and wrong were based solely on what we wanted, then it would be fine for us to eat ourselves to death, drink as much alcohol as we wanted, and have sex with everyone we ever found attractive. Drug users crave heroin. If a junkie prays to God to take away their desire for heroin and it doesn't automatically go away, does that mean it's God's will for them to keep using? Apply this same logic to a rapist. A pedophile offender. A chronic liar or thief. It doesn't work.

4. They are a Christian, but they're just not living like it right now.
This objection comes from the heart of a guy or girl who already knows
they don't belong in the relationship. They are just grasping at straws,
looking for a way to justify the bad decision. Simply put, if they are
not living like a Christian, then how do you know they are a Christian? You don't. They may be faking it to keep you around. Walk away
and don't look back.

5. I can influence them in a positive way. If you use this excuse, then
you are thinking way too highly of yourself. You have an unjustified
confidence in your own ability to get a person to change.

And it never works. The non-Christian always pulls the Christian
down. Charie and I could put together a book of nothing but stories
illustrating this phenomenon. If you really want to influence them in
a positive way, then pray and fast for their soul and their salvation. You
don't have to date them to change them. Only God can change them.
And you may be getting in God's way by assuming that *you* will actually be the one to change them.

**6. Who am I to say I'm any better than they are just because they
aren't saved?** It sounds humble and honorable to place yourself in the
same boat as the non-Christian you want to date by saying you're no
better than they are. And this is absolutely true. But by obeying God's
command to not be unequally yoked, you are in no way saying you
are better than them. You are simply acknowledging the facts. You are
different, not better. You realize that your faith in Christ and their lack
of faith in Christ makes the two of you incompatible. You are heading
in different directions in life and being guided by different missions.
Yours is to glorify God by pursuing Jesus. Theirs is to pursue pleasure,
success, achievement, or happiness without God. That doesn't make
you better than them, but it makes you irreconcilably different.

**7. If I break up with them because they aren't a Christian, they
will be offended by my arrogance and never get saved.** How do
you know that? What if they see your hypocrisy in staying with them

when you're a Christian and they aren't? What if God uses your breaking up with them to show them what a big deal Jesus really is to you? What if walking away from the relationship is the very thing God uses to break them of their pride and sin and cause them to really consider the gospel? It is not your job to save them—and certainly not by dating or marrying them.

8. Once we get married, they will change and start going to church.
No, they won't. If love for Christ and the church is not in their hearts before you get married, it won't be there after you tie the knot. If you were to ask a few people who have married a non-Christian hoping this would work out, you would quickly realize that once the rings are exchanged, all the good behavior and pretension ends, because there is no reason to put on an act anymore. It is a rude awakening when your fiancé promises you they will "straighten up and get back in church" once you're married, and ten years later, they still sleep in on Sundays.

9. Love conquers all, and if we love each other, we can work through our differences in belief. First of all, love doesn't solve every problem. It doesn't pay the electricity bill or put groceries on the table or braces on your kid's teeth (at least, our idea of romantic love doesn't). Beyond that, what do you really mean when you say that if you love each other, you'll work through differences in faith and belief? How do you intend to do that? Will you go to church every other week? Will you read the Bible some nights and the Qur'an on other nights? Or will you go to church and try to follow Jesus while your non-Christian spouse lives a separate life? Does that sound healthy to you? When the kids are born, how will you work through those differences? Will you raise them to love Jesus, while your spouse tells them there is no God?

*

It's better if you obey God. He can see the future and He knows the outcome of being unequally yoked. It causes years of heartache and pain. He wants to spare you from this because He loves you. As

Andy Stanley has said, if we could see what God sees, we would do what God says.

Trust Him in this matter and you will be on your way to a godly, healthy marriage. Don't be unequally yoked with, or tied to, someone who is not following the same God you're following.

Chapter 3

Have You Talked About Money?

T he most tangible, down-to-earth thing that causes marriages to fall apart, according to people who actually get divorced, is money. The statistics prove this.

But Charie and I don't really believe that money itself is wrecking homes. A pile of cash doesn't have a mind and a will of its own to deliberately infiltrate your marriage and wreak havoc on it. Sure, there are *people* who will plan and plot your demise. The book of Proverbs warns about such people, particularly the wayward woman who seduces young, naïve men into her clutches and leads them down a path of destruction. But money is not a person. Money is an inanimate object, like a car or a chainsaw or a baseball bat.

So it's not actually money that ruins relationships. It's our *attitudes and assumptions* about money that wreck marriages.

Sadly, couples very seldom communicate about these attitudes and assumptions. They usually never bring up the way they think and feel about money or how they intend to spend it. Yet these unspoken feelings and beliefs and habits are there, and they cause us to act in certain ways and say certain things that affect other people, especially those we love.

If you don't want your marriage to eventually be in jeopardy, you must talk about money with the person you want to marry. But before that, you have to first come to grips with your own relationship with money. You have to get really honest with yourself. This may be brand-new territory.

A HALF-TRUTH IS A WHOLE PROBLEM

The minute I bring up money with college students and young adults, I hear the same phrases repeatedly (or variations on them):

- "I'm not worried about money. We love each other and that's all that counts."

- "God will take care of us. We don't need money."

- "Money is not my thing. I've never been really good with numbers."

- "There is more to life than money—that's why I'm not obsessed with it."

- "We are putting God first and trusting Him to provide for us."

Later in the chapter we'll come back to these quotes and see why they're dangerous and destructive, even though there is a shred of truth in each of them. These statements betray *attitudes* about money, which we all have. And they radically affect the way we live and how we relate to other people. Especially the one we marry.

Your Relationship with Money

This may sound odd, but everyone has a relationship with money. Even you.

You can't escape it. Even if you hate money. Even if you've never balanced a checkbook. Or owned a checkbook. If you've never even had a credit card or bought groceries on your own. You have a relationship with money, and everyone in your family, your school, your team, your class, even the person you will marry, relates to money in their own way. It's like breathing.

Just like air is a necessity for survival, money is a necessity of life. No one is exempt. Here is what I mean.

You most likely live indoors, not in the woods or a cave. Your home was built by someone with tools and building materials. Those materials cost money. Those tools cost money. Those construction workers were paid. In money.

You most likely eat food. I try to eat at least three times a day, sometimes more. Unless you grow or kill all your own food, chances are you or someone else bought that food from a store. They used money. The food was grown on a farm using seed, fertilizers, and tractors. Seed, fertilizer, and tractors all cost money.

Do you have a car? It cost money. Do you have air conditioning in your car? Do you have electricity in your house? Do you have heat in it during the wintertime? Do you have an iPod, a laptop, a Wii, a Playstation, books on your shelves? Yep. Money was given in exchange for all those things.

And here's one final question. Are you wearing clothes? If the answer is yes, then you have a relationship with money, because it was the means of exchange by which you were even able to get dressed to go out in public today.

So don't pretend that money is no big deal. It affects every area of our lives, both big and small, and each of us has a relationship with it. Some of us love it. Others of us ignore it. Even more are confused by it. But we can't change the fact that we can't do without it and the things it provides for us.

The question is, how do I relate to money and how will this attitude affect my marriage? What basic questions do I need to ask?

Worst-Case Scenario

If you don't get honest with yourself about how you relate to money, then you can never have a discussion about it with the person you love before you tie the knot. If you don't come to terms with how you will handle money as a couple and a family, it may very easily become the issue that destroys your marriage.

The good news is, there is time to tackle this issue head-on. But you should do it soon. Before you wind up like the couple on a date at Outback Steakhouse. These guys were legitimately a worst-case scenario.

Charie and I were on vacation and were eating at Outback in Wilmington, North Carolina. We'd only been married a couple years. We didn't have kids yet, so vacations were still long, lazy days of doing whatever in the world we wanted to do, in no hurry, and in no particular order. Back then we'd go to the beach for a week and read, sleep, eat, repeat. The days would pass in slow motion.

We were also fairly frugal. If someone gave us a gift card, we would use it immediately before it expired or began losing value (or before I lost or misplaced it). We were using a gift card for Outback and, honestly, we were not *trying* to eavesdrop on the conversation taking place at the table next to us. It's just that we were sitting so close to them, we couldn't help it. Okay, maybe we were trying to hear what they were saying just a little bit.

It was a couple who were obviously on their first date. They were in their late teens or early twenties. We could tell they seemed to be attracted to one another. The girl was afflicted with a nervous laugh, the kind that masks excitement and fear. She was laughing at everything the guy was saying like he was a professional comedian. He was eating it up, and the more she laughed at him, the more it encouraged him to tell funnier stories. Charie and I smiled at each other, remembering what it was like when we first met.

Then the conversation took an unfortunate turn. Sensing there was a connection between the two of them and possibly feeling a desire to share something intimate in the moment, the young woman switched gears out of nowhere.

"Well, there's something I want to tell you about myself. It's a pretty big deal," she said.

She was actually telling all three of us, because my wife and I immediately locked in on what was coming next. Was she a CIA operative? A spy? Was this a TV reality show?

He said, "Okay, sure—you can tell me anything!"

He was letting her know that he wanted to know more about her, that he could be trusted, that he was safe to confide in.

She said, "Okay, I hope you're ready for this, and I hope it doesn't make you want to never ask me out again!" This was followed by more loud, nervous laughter from her.

Then she dropped the bomb. "I owe almost $20,000 on my credit cards."

I nearly spit out my Alice Springs Chicken! Charie choked on her Blooming Onion. Then, without any hesitation on his part, he responded like this:

"Well, that's nothing—I'm almost $30,000 in debt with my credit cards, and I have about $50,000 in college loans!"

Charie and I just stared at each other, speechless. I honestly considered interrupting them and saying, "Hey, guys, I think it would be a really good idea if the two of you enjoy the rest of your date and then never talk again. Because if you have this much debt this early in life, the worst thing you could do would be to marry each other. So don't even take the chance. Burn or shred each other's phone numbers and never speak again!"

Of course I didn't say that. But someone really should have warned them. The fact that the two of them combined were $100,000 in debt that early in life was mind-boggling. What on earth could they have purchased on their credit cards that cost that much? Or was it the accrued interest that had put them so far in the hole? Hadn't their parents taught them how to handle money or how to live without fulfilling all their wants?

If those two people did get married, it would be a miracle if they were still together today, not because of the debt they brought into marriage, but because of the attitudes and assumptions about money they brought into the marriage.

They spent money indiscriminately whenever they felt like it.

They both laughed about the crippling debt they had built up.

They seemed clueless about how long it would take them to pay it off and get back into the black.

And to top it all off, they were $100,000 in debt and they were eating at Outback instead of having ramen noodles at home.

Actions and Attitudes

This story perfectly illustrates what Charie and I have learned, and what we want to help you understand.

Your *actions* reflect your *attitude*.

This is true in every single area of your life, but it is especially pronounced in the area of finances. It doesn't matter what you *say* you believe or think about money. It's what you *do* with your money that reflects the truth.

Younger adults seem to always say the right things about money. They want to save up. They want to invest. They want to build an emergency fund. They want to be debt-free and give and tithe and drive used cars and cook at home and cut up all their credit cards and pay cash for everything. Yet the average American now owes somewhere around $10,000 just on credit cards. We can say the right thing without ever doing the right thing.

Again, our *actions* prove our *attitudes*, and our attitude toward money dictates how we relate to it, how we spend it, how it makes us feel, and whether or not it will be the issue that eventually splits our marriage up.

If you told me you loved to run, work out, lift weights, play basketball, and exercise, but you were 60 pounds overweight, always sick, didn't own a pair of running shoes, and hadn't been to a gym or a fitness club in a year, I would be tempted to think you were lying. If we tell ourselves we're disciplined with our money and are going to save up and spend less and stop eating out and cut back on luxuries...while our credit-card statements keep piling up, we may need a reality check. So let's get really honest.

Here's a short list of questions to help you discover your *true* attitude toward money.

1. On your credit cards, do you currently owe more than you make in a month?

2. Do you buy things to make yourself feel better? Do you get a good, settled feeling after you make a purchase?

3. Do you envy the lifestyle your friends have or the things they own? Do you fantasize about owning those same things and having that same lifestyle?

4. Do you eat out more than four times a week?

5. How much food do you have in your house?

6. In regard to entertainment, do you spend over $250 per month on your cable bill, going to the movies, video games, downloads on iTunes, or the latest technological toy? What about your cell phone bill? Ouch.

7. Do you immediately get defensive anytime someone begins to ask for your money—your church, a charity, or a nonprofit organization? This is a sure sign that you actually want to hold on to your money and that you have difficulty sharing your money with others, even those in dire need.

8. Are you cheap when you leave a tip at a restaurant, thinking the server doesn't really deserve the money and you could use it better somewhere else?

9. What percentage of your salary or income do you give away? This could be in the form of a tithe, donations, helping out a local charity, and so on. (Donating old clothes you don't wear to Goodwill or the Salvation Army doesn't count.)

10. Do you ever have an internal struggle before you make a big purchase (try to talk yourself out of it, think of all the other things the money could be used for) or do you spend freely with little regret until hours or days later?

11. Do you fear what life would be like without the safety you think money brings you? Do you find yourself devoting

more time to worrying about the money than being concerned about people who have no job, no food, no health insurance, or no one to love them and care for them?

12. Do you even know how much your monthly bills are, right off the top of your head? (These include health insurance, auto insurance, rent, tuition, credit-card payments, student loans, phone bill, water, and power.) If you don't know this amount automatically, you are in trouble, because it shows that you are not paying attention to where your money goes each month.

13. Could you, in 30 seconds or less, summarize your basic budget? This includes how much you make, how much you save, how much you give, and how much you pay out in bills and payments each month. If you can't, then you don't have a budget at all, even if you claim that you do, and this means trouble in your marriage if you don't address it now.

14. How long does it take you to pay a regular, basic bill? Do you let bills stack up on your desk? Do you open them when they arrive or put them off until after they are past due? How much do you pay a year in late fees due to fear, laziness, or forgetfulness (lack of discipline)?

15. And finally…right now, how much money do you have saved up? Add up what you have in your checking account, your savings account(s), IRAs, life-insurance policies, stocks, bonds, cash in coffee cans buried in the yard, and loose change on your desk. Now, compare that number to what you currently owe, including all credit cards, student loans, car loans, and any other outstanding debt. Which number is greater? By how much?

This list may have caused you some discomfort or even a fair amount of fear. Good—if that is what it takes to motivate you to action. Remember, your attitude toward money forms your spending habits, your spending habits follow you into marriage, and the way you spend money will make or break your marriage relationship.

If you are in good shape, that's great! Keep reading.

If you read these questions and feel like jumping off the roof of the bank (the one you owe your right arm and your firstborn child to), please don't. There's hope for you. It's not too late to change. Not even close!

Back to the Objections

We'll round out this chapter with some practical, doable tips to change your attitudes and assumptions about money. But first, let's return to those lame excuses we've all used at some point when it comes to the way we relate to money. Here they are again, along with explanations of why they don't hold water.

"I'm not worried about money. We love each other and that's all that counts." This sounds really epic and romantic. The kinds of words Leonardo DiCaprio would say to his leading lady in a Hollywood blockbuster. But this statement is simply not factual.

Love is not all that counts. There is much, much more than love to consider. Can you eat love to keep from starving to death? Does the power company let you pay your bill in love, or do they expect dollars? How about the doctor's office? Do they accept love as a form of payment? My wife gave birth to two babies. The hospital billed us for both of them since their employees took care of most of the delivery details, and it was not our gushy, mushy love that allowed Charie to give birth to our children in a clean, sterile hospital room with professionals there to ensure a predictable and safe delivery. At the end of the day, it was our ability to afford good care. You get the point. Love is *not* all that counts.

"God will take care of us. We don't need money." The reason this objection springs up in so many of us is that it drips with religious piety. I used to say this too. And it felt so spiritual when I was 20 years old and boasted I would never own a house or have health insurance (because I lived in my parents' house and was on their health insurance).

I thought that trusting God meant He would bail me out if anything ever went wrong. Now I see that trusting God means being wise, working hard, saving up, and doing my part as a responsible adult to be prepared for the things that happen in life. God does indeed take care of His children—by giving us the faculties and ability to work and the good sense to be ready for the bills that arrive in the mailbox.

"Money is not my thing. I've never been really good with numbers." This excuse is couched in truth for some of us. For many, numbers and dollar signs make their heads spin. But since you can't live without money, you can either continue to plead your ignorance and suffer for it, or you can buckle down and learn how to take care of your finances. What if I said, "I'm not really good at being a dad—it's not really my thing"? Well, I had to learn to be a good daddy. We all learn how to do important things, regardless of whether or not we are naturally inclined to them. We learn to exercise, to eat healthy (most of us, at least), to write research papers, to study for exams, or to get up and go to work when we'd rather sleep. We do these because they are necessary. Handling money wisely is as much a necessity for a good marriage as being in love with the other person.

"There is more to life than money—that's why I'm not obsessed with it." Once again, there is some truth in this excuse. Being obsessed with money is sinful. But having a healthy attitude toward and healthy habits with your money doesn't require obsession. It requires *attention*. Yes, there is more to life than money. But if that is your attitude, your life will be dramatically different (much worse) if you ignore money or fail to deal with it. How does a life sound where you never have enough extra cash set aside to do the following: take a vacation with your spouse, celebrate an anniversary at a nice restaurant, give a friend in need money for groceries, let a single mom move into your spare bedroom, take your kids to Disney World or the beach, or support a missionary in another country?

"We are putting God first and trusting Him to provide for us." A valiant statement! This is something Charie and I strive for daily. But what if you hear me make this statement, then you observe us for the following six months: We stop working. We sit around the house all day and pray. The power company turns off our power. The bank forecloses on our house. We run out of food. Our kids begin to look emaciated. You would most likely confront us and tell us to get back to work, take care of our kids, and pay our bills!

What if we respond that we're simply trusting God to provide for us? You would call us lazy. And that's the point. Many people say this to cover up their basic lack of drive, discipline, or willingness to work. They call their laziness "trusting God to provide," yet they are happy to take assistance from their friends, family, and the government.

Where Do I Go from Here?

We know you want a great marriage that honors God and brings joy to you and your mate for life. That's a great desire to start with. You don't want money to be the issue that kills the relationship. So here are some basic ideas, rules, and mottos that have been tested over time by very wise (and usually older) people. They work, if you begin applying them now (sometimes step-by-step) and continue applying them for the rest of your life.

1. Spend less than you make.

2. Give or tithe 10 percent. Save 10 percent. Live off 80 percent.

3. Make a budget now. Then live by it.

4. Write down your financial goals. Frame them. Hang them in your house.

5. Destroy your credit cards.

6. Try to buy used cars. Don't lease a car, and don't make car payments, ever.

7. Pay off debt deliberately and immediately, starting with the smallest debt and working your way toward the biggest.

8. Pay cash as often as possible.

 9. If you don't need it, don't buy it. Period.

10. Stop eating out.

11. Get a job. Any job will do. Just start somewhere.

12. Sell all your junk. eBay, Craigslist, yard sales—sell sell sell!

13. Be ridiculously generous. Help people in need, and watch God bless you for your kindness.

14. Never, ever loan a friend money, skip work, or buy a time-share.

15. Cancel your cable.

16. Get rid of all the unnecessary features on your phone (and don't talk about being broke as you tweet from your iPhone).

17. Make coffee at home and stop paying five bucks for a cup of bad coffee at a trendy coffee shop.

18. Enjoy free things. The library. Walks in the park. A sunset. Water from the tap in your house, if possible.

19. Ask older couples to tell you about their biggest financial mistakes early in marriage. Write down what they tell you. Read it often. Then avoid doing it.

20. Read the Bible. It speaks of money over 300 times. Obey the directives of Scripture, and dedicate your finances to God as a means to live and support the advance of the gospel.

*

Here it is again in brief: Examine your own attitude toward money first. Be honest. Look at your actions and how you spend your income. Make the necessary (sometimes painful) adjustments to bring your finances under the lordship of Christ. Form new, healthy habits if you need to. Pay down your debts. Stop spending compulsively on things you don't need. Create a budget and stick to it. Be generous and practice giving money away.

Then, when God allows your path to cross with the person you want to marry, you will be able to have an open, mature discussion about the habits and routines and assumptions you both have about money. At that point, you might need to walk away from the relationship, or you may get a green light that tells you to tie the knot. Regardless, you will either have avoided the biggest mistake of your life, or you will have been honest about the one issue that would have most likely destroyed your marriage, which has now been disarmed.

Either way, you win.

Chapter 4

Will You Tell the Truth?

Truth is always authoritative and gracious.
Authoritative words should never be harsh,
and gracious words should never be without power.

Jennifer Rothschild, from *Me, Myself and Lies*

layton and I met in February of 1997 at University of North Carolina, Chapel Hill. He was preaching, and afterward I approached him to ask about his summer camp. I'd been interviewed for many jobs, so when I was hired after only a ten-minute conversation, I was a little surprised. I later found out Clayton had seen me in the crowd and hoped to meet me and make me his wife! So understandably, he was nervous when I stood before him asking for a job. He smiled a lot, repeatedly gave me his phone number, and encouraged me to call him instead of the camp administrator if I had questions. He was dropping hints.

I'd been taken by him when I was listening to him preach. His voice was soothing and he was attractive, but his passion for God stood out the most. I was also nervous to speak to him, but he couldn't tell because I compensated with confidence in my rock-climbing ability, which was the position I wanted to fill at his camp. He looked at my hundred-pound, five-foot-four frame and assumed I didn't have what it would take for such a dangerous activity. But after I'd communicated my aptitude and listed my experience, I was hired on the spot.

Fast-forward to a cool summer night in July 1997. Clayton and I sat on the bleachers at the soccer field at Gardner-Webb University during his Crossroads summer camp, looking at the stars. This is when Clayton initiated our "tell all" conversation. You know—*the* talk?

People may approach how to discuss past relationships in many ways, but there are two ways most people choose.

One is the "tell-all" approach, and the other is the "forgive-and-forget" approach.

The tell-all approach is when you confess everything and leave out no detail. Each person confesses shameful, deep dark secrets, beginning the process of forgiveness. The forgive-and-forget approach is when you forgive mistakes from the past on the front end. The theory is that since a person has already asked God's forgiveness, it's condemning to allow them to resurface. Because God's already forgiven them, we should too.

I tried both methods with different boyfriends. When Clayton started sharing, I realized I hadn't decided which strategy to use when I met "the one." I didn't know how I wanted to deal with my future husband's past girlfriends. Part of me wanted to know everything because I didn't want hidden secrets, and part of me was afraid to dig it up. I was afraid of being hurt.

Before you get married, you need to prepare yourself for the conversations and the resulting emotions that deal with past relationships. They must be dealt with. And here I reveal my conclusion. You need to be ready to tell the truth, the whole truth—and the tell-all approach is the only right way to do it.

The Forgive-and-Forget Approach

I dated a guy for two years in college. We handled a lot of things right, like developing a good friendship for a year before we started dating, and guarding each other's purity as children of God. Our self-control was commendable, but we suffered because we used the wrong approach in dealing with past relationships.

Because my walk with God began at age 11, I was cautious with dating relationships. I'm thankful I was intentional, because I didn't bring many regrets into other relationships. The guy I was dating had a very different history. He had come to know Christ as a college freshman. We met when he was a sophomore and started dating a year later. We had different pasts. He had more regrets and had had less time to heal from them.

When we had "the talk," I shared my regrets and failures, but when I was done, things felt awkward. He looked like he wanted to hide under the table. Shame whispered to him to keep his skeletons hidden. So he asked if I could simply forgive his wild past without going into it. At that moment, it seemed the right thing to do, but looking back, I realize this not only hindered his healing, but prevented a genuine bond from forming between us. He wanted me to forgive things he didn't want to recall. This indicated that he hadn't truly received forgiveness. I should have backed out of the relationship, but I would've felt awful for not giving him what I thought was grace.

In the final days of our relationship, I thought we were growing closer. My transparency helped him share in my fears, joys, disappointments, and victories. But his inability to come clean haunted him. I felt connection, but he felt judged and alone. When we broke up, he said, "I feel like I know you so well, but you don't really know me or where I've come from. I battle with so much regret and condemnation in my soul." Because he was not willing to tell the whole truth, the shame was eating him alive.

James 5: 13-20 says,

> *Is any one of you in trouble [suffering or afflicted]? He should pray. Is anyone happy? Let him sing songs of praise. Is any one of you sick? He should call the elders of the church to pray over him and anoint him with oil in the name of the Lord. And the prayer offered in faith will make the sick person well; the Lord will raise him up. If he has sinned, he will be forgiven. Therefore, confess your sins to each other so that you may be healed. The prayer of a righteous man is powerful and effective.*

Forgiveness ultimately results in healing. If someone is sick, prayers make him well. If a man has sinned, he will be forgiven and healed when he confesses. Ideally this is the way the church should work, but the church often shuns those who openly acknowledge sin.

As a result, many of us have learned to hide sin. Maybe we've tried to be vulnerable, but were met with self-righteous judgment. We don't confess because we don't want to face the scorn of brothers and sisters who are supposed to love us. This fear creates a pattern of shame that can become a lifestyle. Before you tie the knot, ask yourself if you've adopted this pattern. If so, are you willing (or able) to get honest and tell the truth about the things that cause you shame from your past?

A New View of Confession

So, what's the first step toward change? We change our perspective on confession. Confession needs to be regarded as an honorable act of faith instead of a contemptible admission of failure. It's hard to confess, so when someone does we should honor their courage by listening instead of lecturing. It's also important to offer them words of affirmation. Speak to them. Say, "You are forgiven." These words heal.

I take my boys through this process when they fight. I've noticed that when one asks, "Do you forgive me?" he waits in anticipation for the answer. They are vulnerably looking into the other's eyes, waiting to be released. Will they be forgiven? When they receive the words "Yes, I forgive you," they can walk away at peace. If not, they pout. Offer your fiancé or spouse forgiveness. Speak the words.

Second, we walk with them as they learn to overcome their sin. We become partners, friends, true brothers and sisters. How well do you receive instruction without relationship? Behavioral instruction is received much better within a relationship. We listen, encourage, and earnestly lift them up until they are delivered.

Hiding the past doesn't work, because we're putting a bandage over an infected wound. The best thing for a wound is a little soap and water. If it isn't cleaned the infection will continue. So it is with the "forgive-and-forget" approach to the past. We think bandaging our skeletons is more beneficial, but in reality, we're creating a dark chasm of shame that God never intended for us to live in. When Jesus forgives, we are cleansed, no longer slaves to what we've done, because we become slaves to righteousness. Freedom starts when we drag the ugly past out into the light by honest and transparent confession.

> *You have been set free from sin and have become slaves to righteousness. I put this in human terms because you are weak in your natural selves. Just as you used to offer the parts of your body in slavery to impurity and to ever-increasing wickedness, so now offer them in slavery to righteousness leading to holiness. When you were slaves to sin, you were free from the control of righteousness. What benefit did you reap at that time from the things you are now ashamed of? Those things result in death! But now that you have been set free from sin and have become slaves to God, the benefit you reap leads to holiness, and the result is eternal life. For the wages of sin is death, but the gift of God is eternal life in Christ Jesus our Lord.*[1]

The Tell-All Method

So there we were, sitting on cold metal bleachers at the Gardner-Webb soccer field, when Clayton started telling me about his past. I was listening, but I was afraid. I wasn't ashamed about the decisions I'd made in life, but rather circumstances I'd been forced into.

When I was very young, I'd had a stepfather who molested me. I had not been raped, but a part of my innocence had been stolen. Since that time, I'd made every effort to maintain my purity, but I was apprehensive of Clayton's reaction. Would his perception of me change? Would this injustice affect my value in his eyes? I decided to follow his lead. I put my trust in God. If Clayton rejected me for telling the truth, then he was not the one God was bringing to treasure and love me for life.

I shared my story with tears of pain and joy. Although my story is tinted with heartbreak, it is truly one of redemption. I'm usually eager to tell about how God rescued this defenseless child from a life of regret and insecurity. However, sharing this with a man for whom I possessed great affection was emotionally strenuous. After my story, I became quiet, looked deeply into his eyes, and then looked down in anticipation. He reached over, lifted my chin, and told me he was not disappointed or ashamed of me. If anything, he was inspired and amazed.

My story birthed a deeper love and respect for me in Clayton's heart. He saw the beauty God had developed in the life of a girl who could have taken a very different path. Often we lie in bed, holding each other, and wonder how God safeguarded each of our lives. We look at the moon outside the window and ask each other, "*How* did we end up the people we are, with the calling God has given us?" An orphan and an abused girl, married in purity, enjoying a faithful marriage by His grace.

Telling the truth worked for us. It is hard, but it always works.

Trust is both the beauty and fragility of being human.
Our need for trusting relationships is inborn, bred in the bone,
part of the human design. To break trust is thus to assault the
law of life. It is not only harmful, it is a deep moral wrong.[2]

—LEWIS SMEDES, FROM *THE ART OF FORGIVING*

If I'd Only Known

Clayton and I value honesty in every situation, whether in relationships, at work, or in big projects like…building a house. (Clayton says it was the most stressful season ever of his life and he will *never* do it again.)

After our new house was finished, we kept finding projects that were never finished and places where corners were cut. After spending so much money on a home, we were extremely frustrated to find things that were undone or ignored by subcontractors.

July of 2010 was a scorcher in Boiling Springs, North Carolina. The air-conditioning unit for our loft ran constantly. When the temperature inside wasn't cool enough, we thought it had run out of coolant. The repairman who came out told us the dryer vent had been placed too close to the AC unit. This misplacement was causing the lint from the dryer exhaust to blow straight into the filter for the AC. To repair this problem, we'd have to reroute the dryer exhaust or move the AC unit. Both of these options cost money, so instead we chose to remove the buildup on a regular basis. I was thankful the equipment wasn't faulty, but I found my mind filled with skepticism and suspicion.

Questions ran through my mind. Did the subcontractor hide this mistake so he wouldn't be obligated to fix it? Was this an error from lack of planning or simple ignorance? Were we deceived, or was it a simple oversight? As my husband and I discussed the situation, I noticed the phrase "if we'd only known" kept coming up.

If we had known, we could have had the vent moved before the exterior siding was finished. If we had only known, we would have demanded that the dryer vent be rerouted at no expense to us. If we had only known, we would have kept the filter clean of lint and saved the $65 the repairman charged to pay us a visit. But we didn't know.

Have you ever been in an "if I'd only known" situation? I remember my mom wisely advised me to "make sure they take care of everything before they leave because it's impossible to get it fixed after they leave." It's easier to adjust the blueprint than to tear down a wall.

It's no different in building a marriage. When you get close to marriage, being truthful about your sins and mistakes may seem unreasonably painful at first, but it's always easier to swallow on the front end. A truthful beginning alleviates the painful sting that withheld information delivers in the future.

No one likes feeling that the rug was pulled out from under their feet or they didn't get what they bargained for. Deception inflicts deeper, more dangerous wounds than honesty because it plants seeds of distrust and suspicion. Heartbreaking honesty is a way to till the ground in your hearts. It is painful to have our grass, roots, and weeds ripped up, exposing our tender barren ground. However, this fertile ground provides the perfect opportunity to plant a relationship on the basis of forgiveness and affirmation. These are essential ingredients in a good marriage and offer a solid foundation upon which we build emotional vulnerability and trust.

> One of the best wedding gifts God gave you was a full-length mirror
> called your spouse. Had there been a card attached, it would have
> said, "Here's to helping you discover what you're really like."[3]
>
> —GARY THOMAS, FROM *SACRED MARRIAGE*

We Are All Imperfect

If you were fine with the "forgive and forget" method, but are now moving toward the "tell-all" approach, I'm sure you're a bit intimidated. Don't worry. The process isn't much different than salvation. It starts with remembering that no one is immune to sin, and if we claim to be, we are liars. (Take a look at 1 John 1:5–2:9.) I know this seems basic, but when you live with another person your sins start to annoy each other. When you're single, it's easier to camouflage your sins by avoiding people when you're in a bad mood, sleepy, or grumpy, until you get some coffee, a nap, or time alone. Katherine Porter describes marriage as "the merciless revealer, the great white searchlight turned on the darkest places of human nature."[4]

It is not that the institution of marriage itself exposes "the darkest places of your human nature." It's living day in and day out with someone else. I notice it with my kids. I'm constantly saying things like, "Don't forget to speak kindly to one another," "Leave him alone because I think he's tired," or "He didn't mean to make you feel that way." Parents are supposed to help siblings get along, but wives and husbands have to take the responsibility to resolve their own tensions. How do we do this?

First, we remember that our spouse is an imperfect person. With this in mind, we prepare ourselves to expect our spouse to sin. They may lie to you, misunderstand you, make you angry, or frustrate you, but remember, we're still in love with this "stranger" we're married to when the honeymoon stage has worn off. They're the same person you fell madly in love with, only now you get to fall in love with their imperfections as well.

Contempt is born when we fixate on our spouse's
weaknesses. Every spouse has these sore points. If
you want to find them, they'll grow, but you won't.[5]

—GARY THOMAS, FROM *SACRED MARRIAGE*

And so we find another redemptive purpose in marriage, challenging us to love another the way God loves us. Your spouse is not your enemy—he or she is your partner, your brother or sister in Christ. As the great theologian (and musician) Amos Lee says, "Freedom is seldom found by beating someone to the ground." Here is the great irony—when you're pointing your finger at your lover, the darkness of your own heart becomes apparent. Restoring one another in these moments is the goal. Share with your spouse in a spirit of love:

- When you are angry, share what it's about.
- When you are tired or worn out, ask if you can get some sleep.
- When you feel lonely, left out, or unappreciated, ask what made you feel this way.
- When you are disappointed, find out the cause.
- When you're scared by your own selfishness, don't hide it.

Healing One Another

When I feel overwhelmed in my sin, I'm encouraged to know Jesus wants me to find healing. In marriage it's strategically important to remember Jesus conquered the darkness in your mate and wants healing for them as well. Do you want to be healed when you sin? So does the one you love. You're not alone in your conflict with sin, and you're not alone in your desire for victory over it. So God has given you to each other as instruments of healing.

It's important for us to grab on to the perspective that "who we *are* and *what we struggle with* are not the same thing."[6] Did you get that? You are not defined by your struggles and sins.

Let's flesh this out. God created you in His perfect image. But Adam and Eve sinned, and so we all inherit a sinful nature. We are born in sin. But this was not included in God's original design. We were originally fashioned in perfection so we could fellowship with Him and each other. This is *who* you were meant to be. You *are* His creation. You *are* a child of God.

At the same time we struggle *with* sin. However, sin is *not* what you are. There is a difference. I am a child of God, intended to fellowship with Him. But because of my flesh, I may act selfishly or arrogantly or pridefully. However, I am not selfishness, pride, or arrogance. These are some of the sins I struggle with, but they are not my identity as I was created to be.

Let's apply this to marriage. You and the one you're thinking of marrying are children of God. You are designed to be loved and cherished and to fellowship with one another and the Lord. So, when your significant other sins, they are struggling with *being* selfish, unloving, rude, or unkind. They are not the sin itself—rather they are manifesting their struggle with sin.

God hates sin, but He doesn't hate us. So, if your partner-to-be is dealing with selfishness, hate the sin but love the person. When we see our lover through God's eyes, we can find the compassion to help them fight their sin. When we realize our struggle is not against each other we'll come to a place of greater unity and satisfaction in marriage.

Identify Your Identity

We *must* understand that our identity is in Christ if we are ever going to be able to give and receive forgiveness.

When we were dating, Clayton always asked people for marital advice. The most important advice we received came from a man who was dealing with a divorce. At the time I thought his advice was ridiculously simple, but now I understand it was revolutionary. He pointed to Clayton and said, "You must say you're sorry." Then he looked at me and said, "And you must forgive him."

We've remembered those words often in our marriage. Truthfully, we've each had to work hard on saying we're sorry and forgiving. It seems like it will feel better to hold the grudge, or to refuse to back down when you know you're right, but a man can never win an argument with his wife. If he wins the argument, he loses, and if he loses the argument, he loses.

Women, sometimes it just feels good to pull out the list of his failures when your man won't listen. And guys often think, *She's just too emotional to be right. I'm not saying I'm sorry when her reasoning makes no sense at all!* This is the reality of marriage: Men and women listen differently, apologize differently, and fight differently. But we all must forgive.

When we forgive the things forgiving is for, we copy God's own art. God is the original master forgiver. Each time we grope our reluctant way through the minor miracle of forgiving, we are initiating his style. I am not at all sure any of us would have had imagination enough to see the possibilities in this way to heal the wrongs of this life had he not done it first.[7]

—LEWIS SMEDES, *THE ART OF FORGIVING*

God is the master forgiver, because He ultimately understands the effect letting go of offenses has on the heart of the person offended. He chose to liberate humanity through one triumphant, unmatched act of forgiveness. In the cross He released everyone who believes from eternal death. We would have never imagined this plan. He gave His life to save ours.

Humans try to cure injustice with violence, and we try to stop destruction with vengeance. Payback is our greatest victory against crime. But in His wisdom, God uses the power of forgiveness instead of vindication. This is His miracle, and He wants us to follow His example.

The Fruit of Forgiveness

Why? For our own liberation and the liberation of the one we marry. We follow God's example, His miracle, His method of healing wrongs. Why? Because it's His way and therefore it's biblical. Because it works. Because the fruit of forgiveness is sweeter than retaliation. Lewis Smedes offers a few principles on forgiving: [8]

- The first person to benefit from forgiving is the one who does it.

- We forgive people only for what they do, never for who they are.

- Forgiving is a journey; the deeper the wound the longer the journey.

- We do not forgive because we are supposed to; we forgive when we are ready to be healed.

- Waiting for someone to repent before we forgive is to surrender our future to the person who wronged us.

- Forgivers are not doormats; to forgive a person is not a signal that we are willing to put up with what he does.

- Forgiving is essential; talking about it is optional.

- When we forgive we walk in stride with the forgiving God.

A friend shared her story with me over coffee one day, and it beautifully illustrates this truth.

She grew up participating in regular Christian activities. In her teens, she started dating a guy who pretended to be morally upright, but proved otherwise after a few months. Their relationship became emotionally and sexually addictive, and so when she finally developed the courage to break it off, the emotional attachment made it hard to sever the ties. Her efforts to break up always landed her back in his arms. He became controlling and possessive and she felt trapped. So, since she'd already given herself to him, she thought she should stick it out and eventually marry him.

College offered a new start. She began to wonder if she could also begin a new relationship, untainted and pure. She finally broke up with the guy. He didn't take the news well and began stalking and harassing her. Out of shame and to numb the pain, she started drinking heavily and sleeping with multiple men. She was trying to get back at him, but she realized she only felt miserable, dirty, and defiled.

She felt trapped and confused. When she visited home, she wore a mask to hide her torment from her parents. She'd known what it was like to be transparent, to be free with those she loved, but she felt everything was beyond repair.

Finally a casual conversation with her mom gave her the chance to come clean. Her mom happened to ask why she was not with her old boyfriend, and her bitterness and resentment boiled up. She started to disclose years of built-up heartache.

Her mom wept. A new process of restoration began with her mom, but she was still hesitant to tell her dad. This was soon resolved when she and her father shared an intimate conversation as well. She didn't share as many details with him as she had with her mom, but the regrets of the past few years unraveled.

Her dad reacted just like Jesus, the Master Forgiver. He held his daughter in his arms and showed mercy. He reassured her she was forgiven, and the bond between the three of them was again strong.

Tears filled my eyes as she told me about the moment she felt restored.

She was attending her younger sister's purity ceremony with her family right after her confession. When her sister walked to the front to get her purity ring, my friend cried and clasped her father's hand with hers, the same hand that no longer bore her purity ring. She hesitantly peered up at her father's face, looking him in the eyes. She insisted she was ready to commit her purity to God again until marriage. Tears filled her father's eyes as he walked forward with her and placed a ring on her finger.

My friend's story is an ideal representation of the miracle of forgiveness. This father knew his daughter was a sinner. He knew who she wanted to be and knew the regret she felt for not living out her identity. When she finally shared her secrets in the safety of her loving family, confession came through tears, and shame and disgrace were conquered by forgiveness. And she was able to embrace the restorative power of God's acceptance.

Oswald Chambers says that "new life will reveal itself in conscious repentance followed by unconscious holiness."[9] This principle applies any time God's truth enters our heart and forces out the lies that have captivated our souls. Instead of hiding in shame before God and others, we leave our sin and shame behind. The Scriptures tell us about His strong love for us:

> *We know and rely on the love God has for us. God is love. Whoever lives in love, lives in God, and God in him. In this way, love is made complete among us so that we will have confidence on the day of judgment because in this world we are like him. There is no fear in love, but perfect love drives out fear because fear has to do with punishment. The one who fears is not made perfect in him.*[10]

Love and light come hand in hand. Light exposes our faults and love heals them. God sees every fault and loves us anyway. There is no fear in love because His love has covered our sin. We will not be condemned.

Christ exercised unyielding determination to liberate you and me. So we believe He will help us do the same. "God is the original master forgiver. Each time we grope our reluctant way through the minor miracle of forgiving, we are initiating his style."[11] The question for us is, Will we grope? Will we imitate His style? Will we work miracles in the life of our lover by granting and receiving forgiveness?

The "forgive-and-forget" approach may seem easier on the front end, but it brings with it the possibility of mistrust later on. The "tell-all" approach requires more determination and humility, but it produces a richer and greater understanding and representation of the gospel: the story of God who found His people, who were unable to cover their imperfection, and chose to make a way to fellowship despite their filth. We are all filthy and need to be cleansed. Confession and forgiveness heal us. If you want to build your marriage on trust, then you must tell the truth and celebrate the truth. Deep relationships cannot be cultivated if there is a yawning dark chasm that is void of truth.

We wonder if we will be accepted by the one we love once they really know the truth. In marriage, you will learn the answer to this question. It's inevitable that you will eventually learn what your spouse is made of, inside and out. There's no way around it. If you have the courage to ask and the courage to answer, I would bet your future mate would rather know the whole truth before they make a lifelong commitment. Wouldn't you?

Think on this: "If my marriage contradicts my message, I have sabotaged the goal of my life."[12]

May this serve as an example to you as you prepare for marriage. Come clean. Tell the truth about your past. Allow God to restore you. Wait for a mate who will show you the same kind of mercy God does, no matter how wild or mild your past is. Begin with the truth, and you will never regret it.

Chapter 5

Will You Commit?

*I believe marriage is a contract between
a man and a woman to build a life together.
It's a promise to love one another no matter what comes.*

<small>Francine Rivers, from *Redeeming Love*</small>

A number of years ago, Clayton and I traveled to Atlanta to see my extended family for Christmas. I was excited to introduce everyone to our three-month-old son and hear everyone admire his cuteness. But just after our arrival we discovered that my cousin Betsy's boyfriend, Jonathan, had been diagnosed with an inoperable brain tumor and was in the middle of chemo treatments. They received this diagnosis in the prime of youth.

The year before, Betsy was 18 and was attending college in North Carolina. Jonathan was 20 and had just completed hiking the Appalachian Trail. Their relationship had just begun. And now cancer threatened to steal their romance. The treatments made Jonathan miserably sick. Betsy had always been very mature, and I hoped she would find strength in her family and her Savior. I prayed this diagnosis would not embitter the playful, loving cousin I remembered as a child. I asked God to give me faith as I prayed for a miracle.

Fully understanding the seriousness of the situation, Jonathan and Betsy decided to marry. This seemed a weighty decision for two so young, but they had sought the advice of their family. Everyone had approved, and the couple began to plan the wedding. Betsy took off her fall semester of school to help with Jonathan's initial stages of treatment. She resumed school in spring of 2003, and they were married on August 9, 2003. The treatments were successful! Jonathan received a clean bill of health.

Life seemed to be heading back to normal. So, in 2006, the two tried their first round of fertility treatments. But they failed to conceive. That same year their home burned to the ground. They lost everything, including their wedding pictures. Though they were understandably discouraged, they did not let the circumstances of life overcome them. They were able to build another home, and through in-vitro fertilization they now have twins, Hannah and Eli. I remember the day I found out they were pregnant. I cried tears of joy because of God's goodness.

Currently, they live in Georgia with their two adorable children. Betsy is a full-time mom, and Jonathan is working and going back to school to finish his degree. He still has a clean bill of health, and they are thankful. When I think of a couple who embodies the idea of commitment, it is Betsy and Jonathan Booth who come to mind. So as we discuss your willingness to totally commit, we will come back to their story and see how their wholehearted dedication to each other and to the Lord, no matter what, carried them through trials that would have caused many to throw in the towel.

Romantic love has no elasticity to it.
It can never be stretched; it simply shatters. Mature love, the kind demanded of a good marriage, must stretch, as the sinful human condition is such that all of us bear conflicting emotions.[1]

—GARY THOMAS, FROM *SACRED MARRIAGE*

Face Your Fears

Two people notice each other, become interested, and then (borrowing a word from the movie *Bambi*) they are twitterpated. Sometimes this shows itself through silly smiles or stammered words. Clayton and I experienced these feelings when we met, and it led to engagement.

When we announced our status, we noticed significantly different reactions from males and females. The guys would most often look at Clayton in sympathy and say, "Ohhh. Well, I guess you're whipped. Hooked up to the ol' ball and chain." Conversely, for the most part, the ladies screamed in excitement—unless they had secretly hoped to marry Clayton (no kidding, they were lined up in hopes of being Mrs. King when I arrived in his life).

There are always exceptions, but most often guys seem to take a little longer to warm up to the idea of making a big commitment in an exclusive relationship. Girls get frustrated thinking guys are playing the field, but often I think they can't make up their minds and are scared to "limit" themselves. That's why it's so important to understand and face the fear of commitment rather than pretending it doesn't exist.

Everyone reacts differently when making big decisions. Some are comfortable to make them on the spot, and some need a longer time to process. Whatever your style, each person needs permission from their potential mate to go through their process in order to feel settled.

Love can be confusing. Sometimes the passion we feel in love masks that fear of commitment. Our heart skips a beat when we see the one we adore. We get goose bumps and our stomach flutters. Yet in the next moment we're wondering if we're becoming too dependent on them, and sometimes we pull away. So in making a lifetime commitment, we must realistically face our fears and not push them away. Here are some valid questions you both should consider:

- Where do you stand in your relationship now, and where are you headed?

- Are you okay with how the relationship has been going? Would you make any changes?

- What does marriage look like to you?

- Are you ready to dedicate your life to someone else till death? Do you have any fears about this, and what are they?

- Have you discussed your stance on divorce?

- Do you have a game plan for handling disagreements?

- Do you have a game plan for loving each other when the "new" feelings fade?

- What does it mean to love in sickness and health, joy and pain, life and death?

- Are you willing to totally and finally cut off all ties with previous love interests?

Trade In Your Life

Fundamentally, we must trade in the life we currently have for the life we want with the one we love. The rest of this chapter will focus on a few realistic ways your perspective has to change if your commitment is going to last.

We find an illustration of this process in book of Ruth. Ruth is living with her mother-in-law, Naomi, in a region called Moab. Naomi, her husband, and her two sons had moved to Moab during a time of famine in Judah, one of the regions of Israel. Their sons had married Moabite women, but before the women had time to have children, all three husbands died. They were all three widows. This was devastating in this era because women with no husbands had no means of provision unless another male family member was willing to take them in.

Knowing she could not provide them husbands from her womb, Naomi begs them to stay in Moab while she returns to Judah. Ruth and the other daughter-in-law, Orpah, refuse at first, but Naomi again insists. "'Go back, each of you, to your mother's home. May the LORD show kindness to you, as you have shown to your dead and to me. May the LORD grant that each of you will find rest in the home of another husband.' Then she kissed them and they wept aloud."[2]

Orpah decides to return, but Ruth clings to Naomi. She begs, "Don't urge me to leave you, or turn back from you. Where you go I will go, and where you stay I will stay. Your people will be my people and your God my God. Where you die I will die, and there I will be buried. May the Lord deal with me ever so severely, if anything but death separates you and me."[3]

Ruth's words may seem exaggerated for our day and time. Isn't she basically just moving to Judah with Naomi? Yes, they are moving, but they aren't renting a U-Haul and driving down the highway for a few hours. Two women are taking only what is necessary and hiking across deserts and dry mountain terrain to hopefully find family in Judah, if they haven't also faced death from famine. They didn't have cell phones, AAA, or any guarantee of a home once they arrived, if they even made it.

Ruth's future was even bleaker because, as a foreigner, the Jews valued her less than their own slaves. She could be looking forward to a life with strangers who would make her work harder than their own slaves to earn her keep, or they could turn her away. Ruth trades in her life, putting more value on her love for Naomi than on her own life.

Naomi asks the Lord in verse 8 to show Ruth "kindness," but Ruth actually becomes "kindness" to Naomi. The word *kindness* translates the Hebrew word *hesed*, which is basically "that quality that moves a person to act for the benefit of another without respect to the advantage it might bring to the one who expresses it."[4] This is a beautiful portrait of commitment, the kind of commitment it takes to be married.

This same deep dedication is what kept Betsy and Jonathan together in the midst of his cancer. I asked them, "Was it was hard committing to marriage, not knowing what the future held? How did you prepare your hearts?" This was their response.

Betsy: "Jon's parents didn't tell us while he was fighting the cancer, but he was given only a 10 percent chance to survive. We knew there was a possibility he might not make it, but we didn't know it was this bleak. Facing death makes the desire to live that much stronger. I considered being together, facing whatever might come, a better option than staying separated. I could not let the possibility of his death weigh me down. We were equally driven to make a marriage commitment so we could be together for whatever time remained. Trials often tear people apart, but God turned ours into a blessing, creating a more intimate bond."

Jonathan: "I was concerned that Betsy would be a widow if my chemo treatments were not successful. I thought about this for a while before I discussed my anxieties with my dad. He offered the advice, 'If you die before you get married or after you get married, you will still be leaving behind a widow. So, why not get married?' These wise words settled it. Since we had already decided to spend our lives together, I knew Betsy would still feel widowed if I died before we married. So, we made the obvious choice.

"I didn't know if I would live or die, but I knew I was called to keep living in the process. I would not sit on the couch and let the cancer get the best of me. I would pursue life like nothing could stop me."

It's so hard to see the benefits of a trial in the middle of it. Sometimes God allows us to explore the "why's" of His instructions. Other times He wants us to simply obey. Ruth and Naomi, Jonathan and Betsy, didn't know the why's of their situations, but they looked fear straight in the eyes, considered the costs, and made their decisions. They didn't know how their commitments would play out, but they chose honorably and then waited.

Once in Judah, Ruth faithfully gathered leftover grain as the other field workers offered scornful remarks. But she'd made a commitment, so she waited as she labored daily. Then God proved faithful when Boaz noticed her and took her to be his bride and live in his home. Jonathan and Betsy faced sickness, infertility, and a destroyed home. They waited in obedience...then God's blessing came in the form of a rebuilt home, children, and a strong marriage.

I am not saying that facing your fears always ends in miraculous results. There are no guarantees when it comes to the circumstances you will face as a couple. But we need to realistically understand that the feeling we experience when we fall in love cannot carry us for 30, or 50, or 60 years. That will take a deeper kind of love, a stronger commitment.

As long as a couple is married, they continue to display—however imperfectly—the ongoing commitment between Christ and his Church; thus simply '"sticking it out"' becomes vitally important.[5]

—GARY THOMAS, FROM *SACRED MARRIAGE*

Be Wholehearted

Clayton and I were conducting a panel discussion at an event, when I read this question from a student, "Why is it so easy for Jesus to forgive us, when I have such a hard time forgiving myself? What is grace?" I've wondered this also. Why do we feel like it's easier for God to forgive us than for us to forgive ourselves?

Years ago, I wouldn't have been able to answer this question. There were many things I knew God had forgiven, but I couldn't let go of them myself. I kept asking God to teach me grace. After years of trying to prove myself, trying to earn His grace, I gave up. Ironically, this is when I discovered it. I had to change my perspective. I thought grace meant that forgiveness came easy. But actually forgiveness is the most expensive gift we have.

It wasn't easy for God to forgive us. It was torturous. We didn't ache with hunger when Satan offered Jesus bread during His 40-day fast in the desert. We weren't with Him when He got up early to spend some time with the Father before He was swamped by crowds, disciples, and Pharisees. We didn't sweat blood through our pores in Gethsemane. We weren't the ones who committed our lives to death by crucifixion. We can read His story but we will never grasp the arduous struggle of His human will.

It wasn't easy for God to sacrifice His Son. It wasn't easy for the Father to hear Jesus ask why He'd been forsaken. And it wasn't easy for Jesus to carry the weight of the world's sins. When we begin to understand the difficulty of God's sacrifice to save us, we know He paid a tremendous price to forgive our sin. His forgiveness is irrevocable.

Jesus walked away from His heavenly surroundings and gave His life in total commitment to His Father's will for our salvation. His daily decisions were ordered and purposeful. Why was He so committed? How did He fulfill his purpose with such tenacity?

He knew the character of the One who sent Him. He knew the character of the Father, and He knew the Father was committed to our salvation. First Samuel 15:29 says, "He who is the Glory of Israel does not lie or change his mind; for he is not a man that he should change his mind." Our loving God does not change His mind. When He makes a choice, His promise will stand. Jesus committed all His mind, strength, and will to salvation because He knew the Father would be faithful to His promise. God would raise Him on the third day to sit again on His right side in heaven.

We are not Jesus, but we can learn from Jesus. We have Him as our example of total commitment.

Find Your Hope

What are you hoping for in marriage? What if it's harder than you anticipated? Will you continue to hope? Are you all-in?

It's hard to keep this kind of commitment in America, where weddings are regularly annulled and the divorce rate is shockingly high. Here, when we can't make a decision in a store, we remember that our purchase is returnable. Gifts come with gift receipts. If we break a financial agreement, overdraft our checking account, or can't pay our bills, we hire a lawyer to fix our problem. Agreements depend on strategically worded contracts that only lawyers understand. Our mode of thinking is not, *How do I make this right?* but rather, *How can I get out of this one?*

This is the kind of thinking you are up against as you approach marriage because it permeates our society. You won't learn selfless commitment from our culture.

A friend recently told me that his accounting professor said this in class: "In business, if you can steal money and are sure you can get away with it, *do it*! I once had an opportunity to steal a large amount of money and didn't, and I've regretted not stealing it for the last 15 years. It's not wrong if you don't get caught."

We can't let the world entice us. The professor's advice to cheat and lie might work for a while, but soon his folly will be exposed. When we adopt worldly principles, they will poison us to the bone. If we configure our spiritual standards based on sinful, human thinking, we compromise our souls.

Why should we hope for a good marriage in our day? Because God saw it wasn't good for man to be alone and wanted the man to have fellowship with another person. He wanted to give him someone to be by his side, to work with him and share life with him. I think part of God's motive for giving us a desire for intimacy with another person was to lovingly lure us into discovering our need for intimacy with Him. God enjoys fellowship in the Trinity, so He also puts in our hearts a desperation for fellowship with Him, as well as a longing to cherish and be cherished by another person. When we make the ultimate commitment of marriage, we mirror the Trinity: three people in covenant and fellowship (husband, wife, and God).

We must hope in God to give us the strength to commit, and we must guard that hope fiercely.

My son, if sinful men entice you, do not give in to them.[6]

Blessed are those who do not walk in step with the wicked or stand in the way that sinners take or sit in the company of mockers, but who delight in the law of the LORD and meditate on his law day and night. They are like a tree planted by streams of water, which yields its fruit in season and whose leaf does not wither—whatever they do prospers.[7]

Guard Your Hope

Clayton and I were married in the front yard of a beautiful old Southern plantation. It was a gorgeous day, and Clayton says I was too. You might find it interesting that I beamed with excitement and contentment all day, while he was an absolute wreck. Tears flowed down his face the entire ceremony. But he was also smiling, so I believed his assurances that they were tears of joy.

There were three glitches in our perfect wedding day, however. First, a female stalker called our house the night before the wedding and offered to rescue Clayton from me so he could marry her. Second, we couldn't find the train for my dress until I went to walk down the aisle.

But the third glitch was a little more serious. Someone I knew very well and who had been married more than once offered me the consolation that if it didn't work out with Clayton, he would still love me.

This was intended to be encouraging, but instead it stained the innocence of the day for me, like a blotch of ink spilled on my white dress. I enjoyed every moment of my wedding but this one.

When the reception was over and we were headed to the mountains for the first part of our honeymoon, I couldn't get this comment out of my mind. Clayton kept asking if I was okay, so finally I shared my discouragement. He responded lovingly but firmly, saying, "Charie, he didn't mean to discourage you, but we can't take these words to heart. We've made a commitment to be with one another for life, and we also resolved not to discuss divorce. It's not an option. We won't ever talk about it because we're in this forever."

I'm a child of divorce, but Clayton isn't. So, as I listened, I wondered if he could really understand all the "what-if" questions.

- What if he's abusive?
- What if I disappoint him?
- What if, what if, what if...

Then I realized what I was doing, and I stopped and took my thoughts captive. I didn't want to allow a seed of doubt to be planted in my heart, so I quoted Scripture:

> *The weapons we fight with are not the weapons of the world. On the contrary, they have divine power to demolish strongholds. We demolish arguments and every pretension that sets itself up against the knowledge of God, and we take captive every thought to make it obedient to Christ.*[8]

Thinking about Clayton's response to me, at first I felt like it was a little forceful or extreme. But now I see his reaction as simple obedience. He prompted me to aggressively take my thoughts captive. May 1, 1999, on Highway 226, in Clayton's black Ford Explorer, driving to a cabin in Blowing Rock, was the last time we spoke the word *divorce*. The moment that seed was pulled up and cut out of our souls and thoughts, it became unable to grow. My husband protected my heart. He demolished any stronghold before it began, eliminating the option of divorce. The idea was against the will of God for our lives, so we had agreed while we were engaged it would never be discussed. On this day, when the idea tried to surface, to cause doubt, to taint our commitment, my husband fought it, and I joined him in the battle.

Put your hope in God and guard it at all costs. Stand firm and don't be swayed. Don't entertain even a thought of quitting. By God's grace, you can enter marriage knowing it will last until death.

Find Strength in Unity

My cousin and her husband have a unique perspective on commitment because their love has been so severely tested. Here is some of what they said to me.

Betsy: "Love is a 100 percent commitment. We are constantly bombarded with lies about love. The world would argue that love between a man and woman is based upon passion—sex, and compatibility with each other's likes and dislikes. This is only a minute part of a greater whole. I learned that love is a choice. Love is an action word. It is choosing to serve and put another's interests above yours. It is serving when you're too tired to go on, choosing to love someone when it's inconvenient, untimely, and even uninviting. The feelings associated with love are amazing, and passion plays a significant part, but as everyone knows, feelings change. We must not base our commitment to one another, our marriages, on our feelings of love, but on the decision to love."

Jonathan: "Love is not a feeling but a choice. If you choose marriage, prepare for the greatest journey of your life. This journey must be built on commitment. There is no option to quit! I believe marriages are held together by a shared love for the Lord, because we constantly stumble to the cross for help. Strength comes from the Lord. I do not understand His ways but I know He is good. Life came at us hard, but I would have had it no other way than to have had my wife at my side. We constantly help each other on the journey of life. Marriage is an extraordinary adventure."

Unity requires more than one person. If a true bond is to be formed, people must need each other in some way, as do Jonathan and Betsy.

Not all self-sufficiency is negative, of course. When we remodeled our old house, I refused to pay someone to do something I was capable of accomplishing. I replaced the molding in every room—baseboards, door frames, crown molding—as well as the electrical outlets and light fixtures. I installed wood and tile floors in every room but one. I replaced the treads on our staircase.

During this project, Clayton came home one night to a missing staircase, with a stepladder in its place. I had taped a sign to the ladder that read, *"Replacing stairs—be careful when using ladder. Love you."* Clayton often wondered what project I'd be up to next. I was probably a little stubborn, but I saved us a bunch of money. In your marriage, there will be things you will be able to do that your spouse can't do. That's okay.

There's nothing wrong with being competent. The danger comes when your independence keeps you from being able to trust someone else completely. Sometimes life forces us to carry burdens alone, but this isn't God's plan for marriage.

Relying on Another

My relationship with the Lord was solid before I met Clayton, but since we married it has grown immensely because I invite him to take part in my spiritual growth. We haven't kept our "spirituality" a private matter. We discuss our relationship with God regularly and encourage each other with Scripture. We pray and fast together. Clayton offers grace when I'm stuck in condemnation, challenges me in my apathy, and loves me through my imperfections. This is what it means to find strength in unity, and I believe it is one of the most strategic ways a marriage is held together.

Relying on another person feels odd, though. We don't want to be the one who is weak. Inwardly, many of us have always dreamed of having a friend who would love us at all times, who would not leave or betray us, who would not look down on our weaknesses. Then, when God provides such a person, we almost push them away because we're ashamed to be too much of a burden. In other words, total commitment to someone is a stretch.

God created marriage because He saw that it wasn't good for people to be alone. We cannot expect another person to fully carry our burdens because we were "created with a spirit that craves God. Anything less than God and we feel an ache."[9] However, it would be wrong and foolish to overlook God's divine strategy of joining two of His children together in a constant, lifelong relationship based on love. If you are ready, He wants to capture your two souls and weave them with His Spirit to form a cord that will not easily be broken.

A Cord of Three Strands

This relationship, a cord of three strands (you, your spouse, and God), relates to what is described in Ecclesiastes 4:9-12:

> *Two are better than one, because they have a good return for their work: If one falls down, his friend can help him up. But pity the man who falls and has no one to help him up! Also, if two lie down together, they will keep warm. But how can one keep warm alone? Though one may be overpowered, two can defend themselves. A cord of three strands is not quickly broken.*

A marriage relationship that is a cord of three strands will hold fast in hard times.

When I was a rock-climbing instructor, we would tie people to a rope using a knot called the figure eight. This knot keeps the climber from falling by being strong enough to hold their weight. Further, it is designed to tighten on itself under pressure. The more pressure the rope feels, the stronger the knot becomes. It cannot loosen. After a climb, it is more difficult for the instructor to untie the knot than it was to tie it initially.

This is exactly how marriage works. Your knot should always be tightening. The bond you form on your wedding day should be the start of something unbreakable. For many of us, dating and engagement allow us time to live in the clouds and dream of the goodness that awaits us. These are unforgettable moments. But after the calm, there is always a storm. If we are held by a cord of three strands, woven together with and relying on God and our mate, then that rope stays sure no matter what comes our way. It is unbreakable.

Worth the Commitment

It takes work to stay unified. Yet if we stick together, it pays off, and we see God's blessing.

Marriage makes us come face-to-face with our own pride and insecurity. We take the risk and make the vow. We cut all ties with old flames. We walk away from all other possibilities and commit ourselves, heart and soul, to one person. We trust and hope in God to keep us faithful to one another. We lean on Him and each other. We cry and repent and forgive each other. We walk together in unity and give strength to each other when we are weak. And daily, our love grows deeper until finally, our ultimate hope comes true when Christ returns and makes us His own bride.

It is worth it. Are you ready for the commitment?

Chapter 6

Are You Compatible?

Let's play a little game. I am going to mention a phrase, and you decide if you think it's true or not. These are clichés and sayings we have all heard hundreds, maybe thousands, of times. When you read each one, just decide if you agree with it or not.

God helps those who help themselves.
You can't teach an old dog new tricks.
The more things change, the more they stay the same.
If you want something done right, do it yourself.
It's hard to find good help.
You get what you pay for.

There is always an element of truth in a cliché, even if the whole thing may not always work in every situation. We could discuss and dissect each of these and find the ways they are true and the instances in which they are not. But we want to throw one more your way. See what you think about this one...

Opposites attract.

There it is. Agree or disagree? Why?

Let me go on record here and say that Charie and I think this statement is actually true. Who can deny the fact that we are often naturally attracted to the qualities and characteristics in someone else that we don't have? And few if any of us really want to spend the rest of our lives with someone who is exactly like us. What a boring and dull thought that is.

But even if it's always true that opposites attract, is attraction the key to love? Is attraction alone sufficient to build a marriage on? And does attraction maintain its initial strength and energy or does it change over time? And if it does change, does that mean the love you felt wasn't real in the first place?

In light of the attraction you may feel toward someone, you need to ask yourself a seriously important question.

Can I live with the differences that first attracted me?

Or put another way, regardless of how I feel, *are we compatible*?

Let me go on record again here with a bold statement: *Just because you are in love with someone does not mean you are compatible with them.*

This is the essential question in this chapter. If you don't look at the differences you have with your boyfriend or girlfriend or fiancé realistically, you will one day realize that attraction alone cannot sustain a lifelong relationship.

The things you first noticed about the one you married, the things that caught your eye and your heart, will change. Once they change, the differences in your personalities and habits will rise to the forefront, and you will become painfully aware that you married a real person who is very different from you in almost every way. The person you marry will not be a romantic personification of your wildest hopes and dreams. They will be an imperfect sinner just like you, looking for lasting love just like you. And the two of you will be different on every level, starting with your gender and moving on from there.

When that day comes (and come it will!) you will feel either panic—or peace.

You will feel panic if you haven't dealt with the differences. You will feel peace if you did the hard work up front…the work of being realistic about how different the two of you actually are. You may or may not be compatible. You should find out before you get married.

Attraction Is Tricky

Here is a nugget of knowledge that may come as a surprise.

We don't pick what we are attracted to.

That's right—we don't get to decide what our eyes and ears and minds and hearts find attractive. It's almost instinctual to be drawn to certain things. It's what makes us unique among billions of people. For instance, I prefer the taste of Dr. Pepper over the taste of Coke. All the Coke fans who just read that think I am totally nuts. But I can't help it! My taste buds are attracted to one over the other.

ARE YOU CRAZY?

My favorite hobbies are reading, hunting, and riding four-wheelers. There is something about those activities I'm drawn to. But one of my best friends recoils at the thought of getting dirt on his shoes or smelling gasoline. He would be miserable riding trails with me all day. He prefers watching movies or shopping for watches. He is attracted to different things than me.

My favorite color is blue. My favorite food is barbecue ribs. My favorite beverage is strong coffee. My favorite vacation spot is Costa Rica. My favorite sport is tackle football. My favorite movie is *Raiders of the Lost Ark*. My favorite writers are C.S. Lewis, Malcolm Gladwell, and J.R.R. Tolkien. Why? I have no idea.

We are all essentially and fundamentally different. There is something about big tractors I find attractive. You may think that's crazy. But I think it's crazy that you are attracted to a scrapbooking store or an art gallery!

Although we cannot choose what we are attracted to, *we can choose what we do with the attraction*. That's why attraction is tricky. We see something (or someone) that takes our breath away. We pursue it. Maybe we purchase it. All because it looked good and we thought it would make us happy. But once we got it in our hands, it didn't look so awesome anymore. The shine wore off. It didn't give us that feeling we anticipated. Buyer's remorse sets in.

We wonder why we spent $28,000 on a sports car that only two people can ride in. We regret having sex with someone now that the guilt haunts us. You knew you should have broken up with your boyfriend or girlfriend years ago, but now you're married and you think you made a big mistake. In each of these scenarios, what attracted us to something or someone was not enough to sustain us over the long haul.

But the same is not true of love. Love remains once feelings change. Love is a commitment that survives all seasons. And love celebrates the differences that marriage uncovers. Simple attraction bolts for the door once those differences are recognized. In other words, when it comes to marriage, attraction can *get you there* but only love can *keep you there*.

Attraction is tricky because it changes. And often what draws us to someone in the beginning becomes the very thing that drives us away from them in the future. There are some differences you enjoy. There are others you tolerate and learn to live with. Then there are those differences that are nearly impossible to overcome. We call that "incompatibility."

Opposites Attack

At first, opposites attract. But if you are not aware of (and okay with) the differences you have with the person you want to marry, then eventually those opposites *attack*. Let's try to pre-empt that situation by learning how to honestly assess what sorts of traits and habits we can live with for 50 or 60 years, and which ones will eventually drive a wedge into the marriage and split it apart.

What we are advocating is asking questions *before* tying the knot. Make your best attempt to discern who you are most suited for in a mate and what kind of mate would best suit you. After marriage, we're advocating a Christlike humility that is willing to love and accept your spouse for who they are in every facet of their past and personality—a humility that is willing to learn to live with them and love them by God's grace regardless of the differences that may exist between the two of you.

Don't gloss over the major differences that exist between any two people in a romantic relationship. If you ignore them now, they will eventually surface. When they do, they will create some difficult dynamics. Some of the differences will be minor, and you'll be able to laugh them off and learn to live with the tension.

But some will fall into another category, one that's much more destructive in nature. It includes the parts of your personality, your past, your likes and dislikes, even the way you want things done around the house, that are polar opposites to those of the person you agreed to spend the rest of your life with. These differences can become like the sound of fingernails on a chalkboard. And if they're not dealt with quickly, they can create emotional *friction* and ultimately emotional *disconnection*. The end result is emotional *separation*.

Friction, Disconnection, Separation

Here is the vicious progression. A difference in opinion, preference, or habit causes friction. The friction irritates both individuals until they get so frustrated they stop talking. This is disconnection. The longer they avoid communication and stay disconnected, the colder they become toward one another…until they just don't care anymore. Then there is separation.

Friction leads to disconnection, which leads to separation.

This cycle is as predictable as knowing that wind causes leaves to rustle or that rain makes the ground wet. Once you find yourself at one of the stages, the only hope is to stop the cycle by doing the difficult work of talking about the real underlying issues, seeking outside help, meeting with a pastor, counselor, or mentor, and asking God to show you through Scripture how to stop ignoring the problem and start fixing it.

It is totally possible to stop the cycle once it begins. Nonetheless, the progression of the cycle is always the same. Differences always lead to friction. And if you are not prepared to live with, embrace, and even celebrate the differences that naturally flow out of two people entering into a lifelong partnership together, that friction will bring about an emotional disconnection (as well as sexual and spiritual distance) until the two of you are living completely separate lives with no concern or compassion for the other. Charie and I have seen it happen dozens of times.

I had a friend in college. She had two siblings, and they lived in one of the most exclusive neighborhoods in our area. Their father was an executive in a large company and they had loads of money. They entertained guests and had cookouts. Their swimming pool was awesome. The dad drove a Corvette. They were active in a prominent church in town. All three kids were fun, outgoing, athletic, smart, and popular. They were the perfect American family. Or so it seemed.

Out of the clear blue, my friend called me one afternoon gasping and weeping and heaving with sobs. She had just found out that her dad had cheated on her mom. He'd had a secret lover for quite some time. He didn't get caught in the affair. Actually, he just sat down with his wife one day and confessed the whole thing without any provocation. He told her he didn't love her anymore and he was leaving the family for his lover. He would not go to court or fight her. She could have anything she wanted. He would make sure she never had to work another day in her life, and he would pay for college for all three of their kids. He just wanted out of the marriage. Evidently he was either so miserable in the marriage, or so "in love" with the other woman, that he would give up all he had earned and accomplished to get away from his wife and be with his mistress.

Then he sat down with his three kids, without his wife in the room, and confessed his affair to them. They were devastated. He told them everything. And obviously, their question for him was predictable. *Why?*

His answer was simple. He said that over the years, the two of them had grown apart. They were incompatible.

He had become more and more agitated over his wife's habits. He said he had realized about a year after they had married just how different they were in every way, but he'd overlooked it and made it work. But after 25 years, he had all he could take. He cited her love for gardening, which he hated. He mentioned her unorganized approach to cooking meals, which he wanted planned every night. He talked about her love for the beach and how he always preferred the mountains. He loved to play golf, but she hated having his golf clubs in the garage. She smoked, and he was allergic to smoke. She snored, and he couldn't sleep in the same room with her.

He told his kids flat-out that he had gotten so sick of her habits and her personality that he couldn't take it anymore.

Of course, it's easy for you and me to see a man throw in the towel after decades of marriage and interpret it for what it is—selfish sin! He chose to leave his wife. They could have worked through the differences if they had both chosen to. The fact is, he chose not to.

My friend's father went on to say that he and his wife were two completely different people and he had fallen in love with a woman who had more in common with him. He was leaving his kids' mom for a woman he was more compatible with.

What a sad story. My question is simple, though. Wouldn't it have been better if he had paid attention to the differences before they tied the knot? It's *much easier* to work through them *before* than to realize after 10, 20, or 30 years that the little differences you never noticed before marrying eventually wore you down to a place of utter misery.

This man didn't decide to cheat overnight. There was a process that led up to the affair. It started with friction in the relationship.

Friction

Every car engine requires oil to lubricate its moving parts. Without the oil, the parts experience friction and create heat as they rub together, until the motor overheats and ceases to work. A marriage operates in a similar way.

Every single marriage has friction because the two people in the marriage have lots of differences. Disagreements create friction. Kids create friction. Bills create friction. Sickness creates friction. Pregnancy. In-laws. Leaky faucets and unfolded laundry. Every single day that Charie and I are married is filled with some sort of friction, ranging from deciding who is picking up the kids from school to whether or not I need to travel less and stay home more.

Differences in opinion and personalities create friction. In our marriage, one of us is extremely neat, planned, prepared, and organized, and the other one is spontaneous, forgetful, and does most things at the last minute (can you guess who's who)? This simple personality difference is enough to drive us to the point of yelling and screaming at each other if we are not prepared. Without the proper lubricating agent in the marriage, friction creates heat and pain until the marriage ceases to work.

A marriage needs two people who are *willing to understand* instead of *demanding to be understood*. This is the oil in the relationship. It keeps the motor humming along.

If you are constantly expecting your mate to understand you but are never seeking to understand them, your unwillingness to embrace their unique qualities will create a friction that causes the other to disengage until, for all intents and purposes, the two of you stop loving each other and you begin simply tolerating each other. This is the first step down a dangerous and destructive path.

Here are a few things that commonly cause friction in a marriage.

- *Disagreements over finances*: how much to save, how much to spend, how much to invest, how to pay for college for your kids.

- *Differences in parenting styles*: how to discipline and correct the kids, whether or not to spank them or take away privileges or some combination of both.

- *Holiday visits to extended family members*: who to visit, how long to stay, whether to stay in their home or get a hotel.

- *Career issues*: salary amounts, hours worked, late nights at the office, stress brought home at the end of the day.

- *Kids*: how much to spend on clothes, what time they go to bed, what they eat, who their friends are, what school they attend, what sports they play, how much TV they are allowed to watch, who helps with homework.

- *Friends*: how many nights a week you spend with them, whether you go to their house or go out, how to avoid awkward conversations with them, how to avoid getting your feelings hurt by things they say or do.

- *Church*: which one to go to, how to pick one, how often to attend, how much to tithe or give, how much to volunteer, how involved to be in leadership positions.

- *Vacations*: where to go, how long to stay, whether you go cheap and rustic or expensive and nice, whether you get one big room for everyone or two rooms with more space, whether you drive or fly.

- *Sickness*: who cleans the house and gets the kids to school when one spouse is sick, concerns about health insurance, how long it will take them to get better, whether the rest of the family will catch the same bug.

The friction will never go away. We have to learn to live with it. We manage it by seeking to understand the person we are married to and allowing that attitude to permeate every issue that causes friction. If I am loving my wife and attempting to put myself in her shoes in every situation, it decreases the friction. And we move *toward* each other instead of *away* from each other.

But if I'm seeking to be understood instead of trying to understand, the friction gets greater, things get hotter, neither of us is being understood, neither of us is helping or loving the other one—and soon the friction leads to disconnection.

Disconnection

Differences lead to disconnection when we stop listening to each other and caring about each other.

There's nothing sadder than seeing a married couple who is together physically yet miles apart emotionally.

When I was a senior at Gardner-Webb University I went with a friend to Denny's one night to celebrate finishing our midterm exams. We sat directly across from a couple in their 50s. For an hour, neither of them touched their food. They both looked like they had just found out they had cancer. They never made eye contact. They never spoke to each other. They looked all around the restaurant at everyone and everything else...except each other.

I whispered to my friend and asked him what he thought was going on. He said they must have had a big fight, and I agreed. Then as we were about get up and leave, they spoke their first words to each other in the whole time we had been there. I will always remember the conversation.

He said, "Well, is there anything you want to say?"

"No. I guess not," was her simple reply.

"So I guess that means we're just gonna go ahead and get divorced?"

She said, "I guess so, if neither one of us has anything to say."

"Well, okay. We'll have to go see a lawyer first thing in the morning then." And they both stood up, walked to the counter, paid for their food, and left.

The disconnection was palpable. It hurt to watch them treat each other with such contempt. But if you're not careful, you too could wind up in a Denny's somewhere in your fifties, trying to decide if your marriage is worth fighting for or if you should just throw in the towel.

Here are a few signs that disconnection has set in.

- Small, insignificant things irritate you tremendously, but you never bring them up to your spouse or point them out.

- You find yourself fantasizing about what it would be like to be married to someone else or to even have a one-night stand or a fling.

- You begin trying to reconnect with old flames from your past; perhaps you start chatting with old boyfriends or girlfriends on Facebook or Twitter, or through e-mail.

- You get your emotional needs fulfilled through romance novels or movies, or by getting involved in the drama in your friends' lives.

- You get your sexual needs met by watching porn, flirting via the Internet, or fantasizing about memories from your past.

- You find yourself flirting with co-workers, friends, or perfect strangers.

- You automatically snap at your husband or wife when they

try to have a conversation with you or say something you
don't like or disagree with in any way.

- You stop caring about how your spouse feels, and you stop
  sharing small details of your day with them.

- You begin making decisions without their input or without
  even telling them what you are doing, where you are going,
  what you are purchasing, or who you are spending time with.

- You no longer look forward to being at home together, you
  work later, and you look for ways to avoid going home.

Whereas friction is natural and expected, disconnection should not
be tolerated in any form. It must be recognized and dealt with. You
may already see some disconnection in your dating relationship. If you
do, this is a sign that there's something really wrong. You should not
get married until you work through the real problems that led you to
being disconnected in the first place.

Once a relationship lands in the "disconnection" category, unless
major changes are made, it will ultimately lead to the final stage: separation.

Separation

This is the most gut-wrenching, miserable way for a couple to live,
but millions of marriages continue on like this, doing nothing more
than existing. The partners ignore the ugly reality that they are completely separated even though they are still together. The end game of
separation (emotional and spiritual and sexual) is divorce and despair.

The final stage, separation, is close to the point of no return. While
it is always possible by God's grace and lots of hard work to restore a
marriage that has been broken, it is much more difficult to repair the
relationship once the wife and husband have severed all affection and
attention from each other.

Ask anyone who grew up in a home where their mom and dad
fought and argued and bickered until they finally got divorced, and
that person will tell you what a horrible nightmare it was to watch
their parents grow apart until they couldn't even live in the same house.

The statistics are staggering concerning the effects of divorce—both on the kids and the adults who are torn away from a marriage. But we just have to ask someone who has been there. They will testify to the damage done, the pain felt, and the hope that was lost.

I married a woman who had to navigate her emotions through a few of her parents' incompatible marriages. Even as we approach our forties, things that were done and said 30 years ago by Charie's parents still affect her to this day. They also affect me.

You don't want to wind up here. It leaves a giant, gaping void in your heart that takes years to heal, if it ever does. So what should you do?

Avoid the Void

If you want to avoid the void that is left when a marriage fails because of the differences that naturally exist and the anxiety those differences can cause, then you should take some serious steps now.

1. Observe. Pay attention to the small, tiny things your boyfriend or girlfriend does. How does he treat his mom? How does she speak to her father? How do they react when they don't get their way? Don't let the feelings of love steal away your common sense. Watch and learn.

2. Record. Write down what you see. Take notes about their behavior, their habits, their reactions to stress and disappointment and fear. Keep a journal of how their moods change, if they get jealous or angry or irritable at certain times, or if they like to always be right and can never say they were wrong or that they're sorry.

3. Reflect. Ask yourself if the obvious differences the two of you have are things you can live with or if they are deal breakers that make you incompatible. In light of the differences, imagine what life would be like for 20, 30, or 40 years with this person.

4. Invite. Before you tie the knot, invite other people to weigh in on the relationship. Start with your parents, then move to your pastor or another Christian leader you trust, your most trusted and mature friends, and those who know both you and your possible spouse. One thing is for sure—by asking other people who are not "in love" with the person, you will get a much more objective, honest assessment of your compatibility with them than you yourself could give.

5. Pray. Ask God to intervene and guide you if you have doubts about whether or not this person is "the one" to spend the rest of your life with. If you are willing to let God lead you to a decision, He will certainly be willing to stop you if you are about to make a mistake.

6. Decide. Taking all wisdom into account, and being honest about the differences in habits, personality traits, expectations, and family history, ultimately two people have to decide whether or not to walk the aisle together. With God's help and the wise insight of those you trust, make a choice. And remember that this choice is the most important one you will ever make. It affects not only you for life, but also the person you are going to marry and the people who will be brought into being as a result of your choice.

✳

It's worth repeating: Just because you are in love with someone does not mean you are compatible with them. Be wise. Pay attention. And choose well!

Chapter 7

Have You Communicated Your Expectations?

Getting married may be the one event you have most looked forward to in your life. Sure, there are other big days. Graduating from high school. Getting your first job. Receiving your college diploma. Having your first child. Yet no event carries with it as much excitement and anticipation as the wedding day. And as you anticipate that day and the lifelong relationship that will follow it, your mind and heart generate certain hopes, ideas, and dreams.

Ask any teenage girl and she will agree. By age 13 most young women are dreaming about kind of dress they want to wear, what kind of flowers will be there, what song they will dance to with their new husband, the color of the bridesmaids' dresses, and every song that will be played or sung during the wedding ceremony.

Ask any young man and he too will agree, but for very different reasons. Guys anticipate the wedding not because of the beauty and majesty of the ceremony, but because of what they get to do afterward. Frankly, the guy is thinking about the honeymoon. So the wedding is the final step in arriving at his destination.

Because all of us think and dream about the wedding day and what will follow, we also imagine what being married will be like. It's impossible not to! Can you tell a kid not to imagine what Disney World will be like after you've announced the family is going there? Can you tell yourself not to imagine what the Grand Canyon will look like after you've bought your tickets to Arizona? The same phenomenon applies to marriage. We create our own ideas of what it will be like long before we actually get there.

These are called *expectations*.

Every single person has expectations for marriage. We may not know that we have them, but we do. They are there, deeply embedded in our heart or worn on our sleeve in full view of the world. Often unaware, we import these expectations with us into the wedding day and the marriage that follows. But we rarely understand just how powerful they are because we are consumed with excitement of the event. It's usually sometime after the honeymoon is over and the newness has worn off that those silent, unseen expectations begin to reveal themselves. When they do, it's almost always a tremendous surprise to your husband or wife, because they had no idea you actually *expected* them to do things a certain way!

Charie and I hope this chapter will encourage you to dig deep into your heart and uncover your expectations about marriage. You need to think about this now so you can communicate with your potential mate *before* the wedding, not after. If you don't, you may catch them off guard. They may accuse you of being sneaky, dishonest, or less than truthful with them about the things you wanted from them in the marriage relationship (even though you had no such conscious intention).

Communicating expectations is essential to starting a marriage off on firm footing.

The first step is to realize you have some expectations that you probably don't even know are present. They have been formed over many years and spring from many different places, including your family, the parenting style of your mom and dad, your personality, the books you've read and the movies you've watched, your friends and their relationships, and marriages that you have observed from a distance. Having expectations is not evil or sinful. Some of these expectations, however, may be unrealistic or impossible. Let's see if we can dig down deep enough to discover what they are.

"Married and Miserable"

Here is an actual e-mail I received from a young woman (with any details that would reveal her identity deleted). It makes my point perfectly. She has some expectations, not just of her boyfriend, but of a relationship in general. Read this and see if you can uncover the real issues she is struggling with.

> Recently I listened to one of your sermons online about dating...and after listening I knew I should just walk away from my relationship with my boyfriend. I have been dating this guy for a year. He will go to church with me and says he believes in God, but he also parties on the weekends at college and has extreme anger management issues. I love him, and breaking up would be the hardest thing ever. But beyond loving him there is a deeper issue that I won't tell anyone. *I am crippled by the fear of being alone.* I am a senior in college now and all I can think about is how I always thought I would leave college engaged or married.

> In the last eight years, I have only been single for nine months. *I am scared of seeing the word "single" on my Facebook profile even more than I am of losing my boyfriend.* In my mind my identity is in being with someone else...It's easy for people to tell me "find your identity in Christ." But that is so much easier said than done. I have tried. I cried out to God to fix this problem. I got involved in Bible studies, went on retreats, and I would like to say God miraculously came through. But He didn't. I ended up back with my boyfriend, and I told myself that I needed to give up on trying to become closer to God because I was just too far gone for Him to show up in my life. In your sermon you talked about people who have guilt piled on top of sin piled on top of guilt...I have seven years of that. *Not one of my relationships in seven years has been pleasing to the Lord.*

> Last night I saw my boyfriend and I was crying in the fetal
> position and he was screaming...that is my relationship at
> this point. Every day is hard but in my heart *I would rather
> be married and miserable than single and alone.* I know that
> sounds like foolishness but I believe it. I think God is just fed
> up with all my sins for the past seven years and me promis-
> ing Him I will try to change with no results, so He has given
> up on me. I am like the little girl who cried wolf. If I don't get
> help now *I know that I am on a road to a miserable life.*

Wow. This young woman is in a world of hurt. Can't you just feel
the depth of her confusion?

There are multiple layers of problems in this relationship, and it
doesn't take a marriage counselor to see that. The girl is insecure and
lonely. The guy is an immature frat boy. They both seem addicted to
drama. She is afraid. And I bet they're having sex too. I could keep going.

Yet underneath everything that comes to the surface here is one
profound problem, and it lies with the young woman who sent me
the e-mail.

She has some very big expectations from this relationship. And I'm
not even sure if she knows it.

If you go back and read it again, you will see what I'm talking about:

- She *expects* the relationship to give her an identity.

- She *expects* her boyfriend to make her feel happy and loved.

- She *expects* other people to think less of her if her Facebook
  status changes to "single."

- She *expects* this relationship to satisfy her need to belong to
  someone and to feel special and cherished.

- She *expects* to be engaged or married by the time she
  finishes college.

- She *expects* that being married and miserable will be better
  than being single.

- She *expects* a boy to complete her and bring her contentment.

This young woman is not married, and she is already miserable. What's worse is, *she has already decided it's better to be married and miserable than to be single and alone.* I really hope she can pull it together and see her own reality before she ties the knot, because (as mean as this may sound) there is not a guy on the planet who is capable of meeting all of her expectations. Only God can be all these things for her. And that is actually the root of her problem. Her relationship has become her savior. And if her current boyfriend can't come through for her, she will try another guy. And then another one. Each of them will fall short of meeting her expectations because those expectations are unrealistic and impossible.

Knowing the Difference

It is not wrong to have expectations going into marriage. It's just completely foolish to pretend you don't have them at all.

The key is to look at your expectations and know the difference between good, healthy, normal ones and the ones that will drive your spouse crazy because they could never, in a squillion years, live up to them. Knowing the difference starts with some really basic questions. The following ones deal with some normal expectations you need to ask yourself if you possess. Answering these questions honestly will help you uncover those unhealthy expectations that may be lurking in the shadows of your heart and mind.

1. What kind of characteristics are you looking for in a mate? Do you key in more on sense of humor or intellect? Do you look for a deep thinker or a spur-of-the-moment goofball?

2. What physical traits would you like your mate to have? This includes preferences in body type, height, weight, facial features, hair color, and skin complexion.

3. Are you attracted to an outgoing extrovert who is the life of the party or a quiet introvert who prefers more privacy and shuns big crowds?

4. Do you already have an idea of how many kids you want?

5. Would you prefer to live in a big city with all the energy and hustle and bustle and shops, a small rural town with one stoplight out in the country with creeks and woods for your kids to play in, or the suburbs where houses are close together and your kids can walk to the houses of 12 different neighbors to play with their friends?

6. If you're a woman, do you have a desire to pursue a career outside of the home? Or do you want to focus on being a mom and a wife and invest your time in nurturing your children?

7. If you're a man, do you want to marry a woman who is content to be a stay-at-home mom? If your wife wanted to work part-time or full-time outside the home, would that bother you? Would that be a deal breaker?

8. At what point in your marriage do you hope to start having children? Do you want to wait for several years? Do you want to start immediately? Or have you decided you don't really know if you want children at all?

9. Do you have an expectation of where you want to live geographically? Do you want to live close to your parents and your extended family or close to where you went to college? Do you already have your heart set on a particular region or city?

10. What kind of church do you expect to attend and raise your kids in once you get married?

The list above should begin to unravel your subconscious ideas of what the ultimate marriage looks like.

Exposing Your Hidden Expectations

Growing up, we eventually mature to the point of understanding that the solar system, including the Earth, revolves around a medium-sized star called the sun. When that reality sets in, it may help us recognize certain implications: We also are not the center of the universe, which naturally means we won't get everything we ever wanted out of life.

This is an essential realization. Unfortunately, some people never get it. If you import a self-absorbed, self-centered, self-serving perspective on life into your marriage, you will make two people extremely miserable (you and your unlucky spouse).

IN YOUR DREAMS!

Let's face it...there are some things we may hope for in life that just ain't gonna happen. Ever.

- You will not get to sleep till noon every day and have your wife serve you breakfast in bed.

- Your husband won't arrive home from work every day on a white stallion, holding a dozen roses, with his chiseled chest jutting out from an unbuttoned shirt.

- Your wife will not be okay with you watching SportsCenter three times, back to back to back. Every day.

- Your husband may get a gut, or go bald, or both.

- Your children won't turn out like the Cosby kids.

- You will *never* have sex as often as you did on your honeymoon.

You get the point, right?

If you looked at the tongue-in-cheek list above, I hope it prepared you to look at some *serious* unrealistic and impossible expectations that, honestly, nobody could live up to. As mentioned, they will drive your spouse nuts as well as cause you major disappointment when your mate can't live up to them:

1. Believing that you and your spouse can immediately enjoy a lifestyle equivalent to that of your parents, even though it

took them 30 years of marriage to give you the lifestyle you had when you lived with them.

2. And similar to #1, expecting immediate financial stability with plenty of money in the bank to pay for vacations, a new house, a new car, new furniture, and new appliances and accoutrements.

3. Thinking that you both will always have the energy and desire to travel and play and do the things you did when you were dating, when you had few or no responsibilities.

4. Hoping for a home-cooked meal every evening as soon as you walk in the door from work.

5. Believing that your husband will automatically want to (or know how to) help out around the house with the laundry, the dishes, mopping, vacuuming, scrubbing toilets, and dusting.

6. Hoping that your wife will want to have sex with you every day, every night, or every day and every night like you did on your honeymoon.

7. Dreaming that your husband will pursue you with romantic overtures, poems, handwritten cards, flowers, and candlelight dinners every day like he did when you first met.

8. Anticipating that your spouse will want to go see your family often or want to invite them to your house for holidays and special occasions.

9. Thinking that you will both agree on how to decorate the house, arrange the furniture, paint the walls, place the trash can, share the toothpaste, place the TV, arrange the bookshelves, hang the pictures, sort the mail, park the car, use the computer, organize your closet, cut the grass, buy groceries, work out at the gym, and take vacations.

10. Imagining that you will naturally want to spend money the same way on the same things.

So what happens if both the guy and the girl enter into the marriage covenant having never talked about what they expect from the other one? Do you think all the expectations just disappear once the vows have been repeated and the rings exchanged? No way! They are still there. And they will make themselves known very quickly.

Then, your spouse will either embrace them and attempt to adjust their habits to your desires, or they will reject them. Our human nature is selfish—therefore most of us get extremely defensive as soon as anyone expects anything from us. Your default mechanism will cause you to recoil at giving up your rights and dreams in order to fulfill some need your spouse has or some expectation they throw on you. That is usually when the fireworks start. You see, marriage is not for the faint of heart! It's for grown-ups who are willing to work at putting the other person first while putting their own desires on the back burner.

Marriage is a mechanism God designed to expose the real you. It forces you to live in the same house with another adult you're not related to by birth. And as the two of you collide on a daily basis, you begin to see that you have certain habits and specific ways of looking at life and doing things—and that your mate does not have those same habits. They see things and do things differently than you do. You are two very different and unique people who could, if you don't do things right, get on each other's nerves, drive each other insane, or aggravate one another to the point of divorce.

No Smuggling

Enjoy all the surprises during the dating phase and the engagement, but don't smuggle any surprises into the marriage. Get these things out in the open. Lay them on the table, and don't be shy, afraid, or embarrassed to share the things that you have always dreamed about and hoped for in your marriage.

Who knows? Your fiancé may deliver all your expectations and more. Or they may not be able to give you any of what you had hoped for. But you will never know unless you talk about it. And that means *all* of it. If you have some impossible expectations, at least they can tell you "no way!" before you tie the knot. Then you can decide if you're able to let go of some of your expectations and take your potential mate as they are, or that something is a deal breaker and you need to call the whole thing off.

One important thing that this kind of conversation will do is remove the anxiety of the unknown. It takes away the element of unpleasant surprise. Both of you can come together in an attitude of mutual trust and share intimate and personal dreams for what you want out of marriage.

Maybe you understand the need to address each other's expectations, but confrontation terrifies you. You aren't used to bringing up sensitive subjects, and you need help. If you feel this way, it would be good to start practicing now because such issues will always exist. They will always need to be discussed in relationships, and marriage does not lessen this need. Rather, it makes the need greater.

So here's a practical approach we saw a couple we admire take. They purchased a book containing pages of both deep and more superficial questions. They would bring the book on dates and ask each other a few questions each time. Issues like where to spend the holidays, how they liked to be cared for when sick, or how many children they hoped to have one day. The book also contained spiritual questions. It took away the pressure to bring the questions up, but it allowed the couple to discuss them—because if the book asked it, they had to talk about it.

When you begin to talk about your expectations, as said earlier, often you will realize that some of them are practical and attainable while others are just never going to happen. They come true in the movies but not in the real world where you live. Then you are able to shorten your list. You can whittle it down to something that your boyfriend or girlfriend can actually work on and achieve. And beyond all the things on your list, you have just established a level of trust and open communication, both of which are necessary elements in a healthy, God-honoring marriage.

A Word of Caution About "The Talk"

When you are sitting down together and the person you love is pouring their heart out to you in total vulnerability, be aware of how you respond. Use care with your words, your body language, and your facial expressions. You don't want to shut them down or make them feel stupid if they share some things that sound insane to you. Here is a word from our hearts to yours that we believe will help you not make your future spouse cry.

Some good things to say:

- "I'm so glad you feel comfortable telling me this."

- "This is a really good conversation for us to have right now."

- "I really want to know what you want and need from me in our marriage."

- "This is so important to me, I thought I should take notes and write down what you say. I don't want to forget anything you share."

- "Tell me everything! Don't hold anything back. I want to know everything you're feeling."

- "Don't feel selfish when you share your expectations with me. I want to serve you and help bring you joy in our marriage."

- "I will do the best I can to learn your heart and your habits and to listen to you when you tell me what you need and how you feel."

Some bad things to say:

- "How long is this gonna take?"

- "I'm pretty stubborn so I hope you're not expecting a whole lot of change from me."

- "Let's just let go of all our expectations and figure this thing out as we go, okay?"

- "I hope your list of expectations is pretty short, 'cause I'm gonna be so busy at work once we get married."

- "There is no way I can do all of that. Actually, there's no way I can do half of the stuff on your list!"

- "Just tell me that you're not expecting me to be like your mom, because I can't stand her and I will never be like her."

- "If you're expecting me to be like your dad, you might as well give up on that. I am totally different than him."

- "Are you crazy?"

No Secrets

Remember—it's not your expectations that will harm your marriage. It's your *secret* expectations you need to be concerned about.

If you act as if love will conquer all future problems and refuse to admit your expectations, you will find yourself in serious trouble. Maybe not today. But one day. If you are willing to come face-to-face with what you want out of a marriage, and then you honestly communicate that with the person you believe God has called you to spend your life with, you are much more likely to have a God-honoring, Christ-centered, healthy marriage.

Charie and I had been dating for a few months, and I knew way before then that I was going to marry her. I also knew that she was aware of my calling to preach the gospel (after all, we had met at an event where I was preaching). But I also wanted to be totally up-front with her. No surprises. I wanted to specifically spell out what God had called me to do and what I thought being married to me would be like. So one night as we sat in my driveway I decided to lay all my cards on the table.

The conversation went like this...

"Charie, I need to tell you, before we go any further or talk about marriage, that when I was 14 years old, God called me to preach the gospel and I said yes. I have dedicated my life to working with and serving people. I will always be an evangelist. I will always travel and tell people about Jesus. And if you can't handle that, or if you're not sure that you can live with a man like that, then we need to have a serious conversation about our future and whether or not this will work out."

I felt smug and confident and really spiritual at that moment. I was pretty sure there was a golden glow around my head, probably a halo.

Charie's response floored me. It was the last thing I expected to hear from her, but it was the most profound and wonderful thing that could have possibly come out of her mouth at that moment.

"Well, thanks for telling me that. But you need to know that when I was 12 years old, God called me into ministry. I told Him I would serve wherever He led me. So you need to know that I'm not going to just sit at home while my husband serves God. I will be his partner, and I want to serve with him where God sends us. I hope you are okay with that."

Boom. And yes, I was okay with that. I still am. And I always will be.

So be wise and do the hard work now. Here are a few practical steps that summarize what you've read in this chapter.

1. Pray to God for insight into your own heart, asking Him to reveal secret desires you may be unaware of.

2. Ask your parents, grandparents, and other trusted family members what kind of mate they see you marrying, and what characteristics they think your spouse will need in order to meet your expectations.

3. Make a list of the expectations you have that you will not give up or compromise on. These are the essentials—and you will not, under any circumstances, marry someone who doesn't meet the list.

4. Make another list of the expectations you have that are impossible, unrealistic, unattainable, or silly. Be willing to let go of these and lay them aside.

5. Keep a prayer journal and record some of the prayers you pray for your future wife or husband. Then after marriage,

let them read those prayers. That will be a meaningful (and possibly passionate) moment for the two of you.

Charie and I pray that you can enter into the most fulfilling relationship in all of life with your eyes wide open and your expectations on the table…with no surprises. It will work, we promise.

Chapter 8

Are You Ready to Marry an Entire Family?

"I'm marrying them, not their family."

When people say this, they need to realize that nothing could be further from the truth.

When you tie the knot, you are not tying it with just your husband or your wife. You are actually tying it with their immediate family. You are tying it with their extended family as well. Furthermore, you are tying the knot with the person your mate will be in the future—and with the person they are because of the cumulative history that took place in the context of their family. Their identity and personality were composed and cultivated by the people they grew up with. That means their family made them who they are. And your family made you who you are.

In a nutshell, your family is the greatest contributing factor to *why* you are *who* you are.

Our families are the source of our values, likes and dislikes, belief systems, traditions, expectations, habits, memories, and future hopes and goals. And when you get married, you are buying into the cumulative history of your mate's family as they have helped form and shape him or her. Your mate is doing the same exact thing by marrying you.

Charie and I want to make this clear, just in case you've bought into the cute little idea that you can marry someone without marrying their family. Even if the immediate or extended family lives in another state, or even another country, you are still inheriting that family by extension, because (to put it in one phrase) that family and all their traits and traditions live within your spouse.

No Exceptions

The thought has probably crossed your mind, even as you were reading the paragraphs above, that there are exceptions to this rule. With very little effort, you think, you could come up with a list of scenarios where this principle would not apply. Because I'm a fairly nice guy (at least my dog thinks so), I would like to save you some trouble and go ahead and give you the list right here.

You may think that these situations prove you can marry someone without marrying their family. But they don't.

1. What if he and his parents don't get along at all and they disagree on politics, religion, and all other important things?

2. What if her parents are completely different than her, with different ideas about marriage and life and the future?

3. What if there was a major disagreement or fight in the past and there is almost no chance they will ever patch it up, or maybe even ever speak to each other again?

4. What if they live so far away from their parents that it will make it nearly impossible to ever see them, even for a holiday visit?

5. What if their parents were much closer to one of their siblings? Doesn't that mean they will have more influence on the brother or sister than my future mate?

6. What if he comes from a dysfunctional family and has sworn to never follow their example or how they did things at home?

7. What if her parents have declared they want to let the two of us make our own decisions and have promised to keep their noses out of our business?

8. What if they had a mom and a dad and a stepmom and a stepdad? Shouldn't that be too many people to really have any lasting influence on the way they see life and do things?

9. What if I can already tell that they are so fundamentally different than their parents that there would be no way they would turn out like them or bring their habits and traditions into our marriage?

10. What if they grew up far removed from their grandparents, aunts and uncles, and cousins? Doesn't that mean that the only real family influence they had was their mom and dad?

We've heard all of these reasons used by lovestruck couples as proof they didn't need to pay attention to or do any real research into the family background of the person they wanted to marry. In my case, I've begged every single one of those couples to reconsider and spend some time getting to know the family of the person they love before they jumped right into marriage. Some have taken my advice. Some have not. Some of those marriages have ended. Some are still together. And while I pray and believe that they will continue to survive, only time will tell.

Everyone becomes who they are because of the family that raised them. There are no exceptions. It could be a traditional family with a mom and dad who love each other and provide love and support for every member. It could be a divorced family complete with stepbrothers and stepsisters. It could be a foster family, an adopted family, a friend's family, a great big extended family, or even a family at an orphanage or a group home. Regardless, we all have to grow up, and we all grow up somewhere.

Your future mate will come into your marriage as a unique individual, with no other person like them on earth. The same is true of you.

And as you begin a life together, you will inherit their traits and idiosyncrasies and habits and expectations. They are all part of the package, and they all come from the way your spouse was raised.

The problem occurs when the man or the woman is not willing to prepare themselves mentally and emotionally for the inevitable day when they realize that their mate is saying or doing things that they don't like, and the things they are doing are exactly like the things their mother or father used to do.

The good news is, your marriage can be an incredible experience of love and service and joy despite the differences in how the two of you were raised. Every marriage that turns out well is proof of this, because every marriage by definition includes two people who come from different families and contexts and cultures with different views and values. When those two people understand the sacrifices required to make marriage work over the long haul, each embraces the other, along with all the residual effects of the family the other came from.

NATURE AND NURTURE

Charie and I believe it's a combination of both nature and nurture that makes you, and your mate, who you are. You need to recognize the roles of both in the development of your personality traits. And just like you were formed as a result of the DNA you were born with and the nurture you were given, in the same way, your husband or wife was also influenced and formed by both forces.

We also believe it's critical that you understand this confluence of forces before you tie the knot so you are equipped to better understand the behavior, attitudes, and reactions of your spouse (and yourself) once you're married. Remember, the person you are marrying was formed and developed by a family, but they were also uniquely designed by God. In your mate you see their relatives... and their Creator.

Three Arenas

The older someone gets, the easier it is to see them becoming more and more like their mother or their father. Age seems to bring out the similarities we all have with our parents, even though we may never before have seen any common traits.

I observed this with my own mother. Her dad (my grandfather) was always obsessed with time. He hated being late. He would show up two hours before a doctor's appointment. If I told him I would come over to help him cut the grass at 2 p.m., he would call me at 10 a.m. to make sure I was ready. I'm not kidding. It sounds cute, but it was quite aggravating.

As my mom got older, about the time I was in high school I began noticing her obsession with being early to everything. She would be ready hours before an appointment. When I finally got a cell phone, she would call me when I was driving home for a visit, wondering where I was and when I would arrive, even though it was still three hours before the time I was supposed to get there. My dad saw it too. He lived with her. He would constantly joke about it. One Monday afternoon, for instance, he said to my mom, "Jane, you better be heading on to the doctor's office. Your appointment is Wednesday at three and it's really going to push you to make it on time!" He would die laughing. She would give him a mean look. She had become exactly like her own father.

There are three arenas of life where the shaping and forming of family becomes evident: behavior, attitudes, and reactions. So pay attention to these in yourself as well as in your future mate.

Behavior

It makes sense that a majority of our behaviors are learned from the people we spend most of our time with. And during our most formative years, most of our time is spent with our family. By the time we become teenagers, we are spending more time with our peers and friends, but by then most of our thought patterns and behavior patterns are already shaped and solidified.

Our pediatrician told us that our boys would have the basic building blocks of their personalities in place by the time they were five years old. This means that whoever has access to a child for the first five years of their life gets to influence the building blocks for the actions and attitudes that child will demonstrate for the remainder of their days on earth. Then until the age of 18 or so, that young man or young woman lives in a house with parents and perhaps brothers and sisters and learns how to act in the context of those relationships.

So as you observe the behavior of the person you love and want to marry, you may want to consider doing these things.

1. Be deliberate in spending time with their family so you can see how they interact with them at their home.

2. Be mindful of your own behavior patterns and honestly assess which behaviors are acceptable and which ones are not. Then repent of any behavior that doesn't honor Christ or would be destructive in a marriage.

3. Don't gloss over any behaviors you see in your boyfriend or girlfriend that would be major red flags in a marriage. Write them down and talk about them. They could be deal breakers.

4. Let the Bible be the standard for acceptable behavior in your life, and demand that it also be the standard for the one you wish to marry. If they don't agree or don't submit to Christ and His will as revealed in Scripture, then you should walk away. (See chapter 2, "Are You 'Equally Yoked'?")

Here are some behaviors that you should immediately take notice of. By God's grace, they can be corrected, but don't wait till *after* you get married. If you see most of these traits in yourself or the one you love, you may need to call off the relationship. Some warning signs are that he or she…

- has a tendency to yell or raise their voice anytime they are frustrated

- has a history of short relationships

- has a history of numerous relationships
- currently struggles with an addiction to porn
- currently struggles with drug abuse
- currently struggles with alcohol abuse, getting drunk, or binge drinking
- has a track record of sexual sin with every previous love interest
- is always involved in some sort of drama
- is often involved in other people's business
- constantly gossips, spreads rumors, or creates controversy
- fights and argues with parents
- never has any money and is always broke
- is always behind on paying their bills
- is always late, often fails to show up for appointments
- has no job or cannot keep a job for very long
- has a history of starting things and not finishing them
- plays hours of video games every day
- spends lots of money on clothes, entertainment, music, or cars
- is not involved with and dedicated to a local church
- is easily offended when confronted with their own sin
- is lazy, lethargic, apathetic; sleeps late every day
- stays up late playing video games, watching TV, or surfing the Internet
- says outlandish things or posts questionable pictures on Facebook, YouTube, or other social media
- curses and swears frequently

- tells inappropriate jokes about sex

- talks down to people, cuts people off in conversations

These are major red flags, and you'd better pay attention to see whether you or the person you want to marry displays any of these. Don't fool yourself. You do *not* want to marry someone while telling yourself, *They will change once we get married.* This is a guaranteed disaster in your future, and you should run the other way if you ever say that to yourself.

Pay attention to their behavior. Pay attention to your own.

Attitudes

We *act in certain ways* because we have *attitudes about certain things*. Our attitudes precede our actions, and our attitudes were shaped by our family of origin.

But don't get the impression that we can blame someone's sin on their family. This is not the case at all. Everyone must take responsibility for his or her own actions. Keep that in mind as we look at how attitudes can be even more hurtful and destructive than actions.

Our actions reflect our attitudes and always flow from them.

For instance, say you're interested in a guy but you notice he always speaks disrespectfully about women. His behavior may be repulsive, but it flows from a negative attitude toward women. (He may have picked it up from his dad or grandfather, or maybe from friends at school or too much TV.)

If you are dating a young woman but notice she constantly criticizes herself (her figure, her hair, her complexion, her weight), her self-critical actions point to an attitude of insecurity. Her actions reflect her attitude.

And here's one more example that Charie and I see all the time. If you are in a relationship with someone, but you often notice they become withdrawn, sullen, and sad, the behavior they display may simply look like pouting. Yet their underlying attitude may be a strong self-centeredness that cannot stand not being the center of attention. The pouting is a way to get you to notice them and to get your undivided attention. The attitude behind it is selfish pride. Again, our actions reflect our attitudes.

Observe the attitudes underneath some of the following actions in you and the one you desire to marry. Does your boyfriend or girl-friend (or do you)…

- have an extremely judgmental attitude toward other people?

- always play the role of the victim?

- believe that other people are "out to get" them all the time?

- constantly complain about everything?

- treat waitresses, cashiers, custodians, or other people in service roles with contempt?

- find something negative in every situation regardless of how many positive aspects there are?

- ignore the feelings of other people?

- show insensitivity in your relationship by ignoring simple requests or refusing to listen to your concerns?

- always promise to "do better" if caught or confronted in a sin, but never follow through with the promise?

- blame other people for their own failures?

- bring up past relationships often?

- flirt with others in front of you?

- spend money carelessly, have no budget, and refuse to talk about finances?

- always take over conversations and turn the attention back to themselves?

- become plagued with jealousy when someone else succeeds at anything?

One or two of these red flags don't automatically mean you need to run for the hills and get a restraining order. If the person who displays these attitudes is willing to admit their sin, repent, and seek godly help from older, wiser Christians, then you can stay in the relationship. But if they show no willingness to leave the destructive patterns they've fallen into, then you must walk away.

Reactions

The final arena you should pay close attention to is the way your possible future mate (or you) reacts to certain important things. The way people respond to stress, anxiety, disappointment, and contentious situations is—as with other things—a combination of their own personality and the reactions they observed growing up in their parents' home.

I've seen this in my own life. My father was a farmer, and I was his helper. When he was working on a tractor or a fence line and something broke or went wrong, he would take off his hat and throw it on the ground. He wouldn't curse or yell, he just threw his hat down.

Recently I was out in our yard with my sons, planting some maple trees. I was digging the holes by hand with a mattock and posthole digger, when I hit a gigantic rock. I worked and worked to break through it, and as I was trying to pry it out of the ground, the wooden handle on the mattock cracked. I was hot and sweaty and frustrated, and I did something without even thinking about it...I took off my hat and threw it down on the ground.

It was right then I realized I had just reacted to a frustrating situation in the exact same way I had seen my dad do it throughout my childhood and adolescence.

So be mindful and attentive to reactions you see in the person you intend to marry, whether they come from family influence or inborn personality. Here are some negative, unhealthy patterns of reaction to watch out for:

- a quick temper that is easily ignited when things go differently than anticipated

- a tendency to speak loudly in order to manipulate others or force them to listen

- facial expressions or other nonverbal communications that show disdain or impatience

- critical, judgmental comments in response to the blessings or successes of other people

- an immediate need to blame personal failures or bad decisions on someone else or some other factor

- emotional outbursts in social settings where they are not the center of attention

- defensive posturing anytime they are confronted about issues in their life, whether big or small

- an unwillingness to humbly listen to your perspective on an issue on which you disagree

- getting angry and holding on to that anger instead of letting it go, seeking forgiveness, or actually talking about the issue that upset them

As you move into the most important relationship of your life, remember that long after your mate's parents are dead and gone, the values and virtues, attitudes and actions that they passed on to your husband or wife will live on.

The same is true for you and your family. You will carry forward the DNA, the habits, and the reactions you learned from your family. The great joy of marriage is leveraging those differences for your advantage as you learn to love and serve one another despite the differences, creating your own family with your own values, beliefs, habits, and legacies to pass on to the next generation.

Chapter 9

Are You Willing to Submit?

C layton walked into the room with a package in his hands. I didn't know what he was holding, but I was hoping it was for me. We'd recently had a conversation about ways he could express his love to me. I asked if he could start thinking about bringing home little gifts, tokens of love. To me, this was tangible evidence that in his absence he had not forgotten me; proof that I remained in his thoughts. The gift did not have to be exorbitant, maybe a pair of earrings or a latte from the local coffee shop. When he brought something home, it felt like a declaration of love.

But as he came in the room, he was wearing a weird expression. His face was hesitant. It seemed to say, *I've got something for you, but I'm both excited and scared at the same time to give it to you.* I thought maybe he was upset about something, so I told myself to remain calm. I watched and listened as he explained, "I have something for you, but I didn't pick it out myself. It's a book my friend recommended because he and his wife said it changed their lives. So I thought I would get one for us."

He continued, but I tuned out. I couldn't focus because my heart started beating faster and faster. My mind nervously scrolled through the entire week's phone conversations. I tried to pinpoint something I'd said, anything that might have hurt his feelings. In my recollection the week had gone well, so I sat there confused.

I noticed his voice in the background and realized he was still talking, but the words sounded to me like those of Charlie Brown's teacher. I refocused and tried to listen again. He was apologizing for my gift.

My gift? Yes, he got me a gift. What? He's apologizing? What is he saying? "You are not a disrespectful wife," he explained, "and I know you appreciate me, but our friend said this book was so good for their marriage, and I thought it might be good for us too. I just wanted to find something we could read and study together."

Okay, so now my heart was really beating and my body temperature was definitely rising. A feeling of insecurity and condemnation flowed down my spine, in the form of perspiration. *He just said the book helped their marriage? Oh, no—is something wrong with our marriage? What's going on? Is he unhappy? I had no idea… Wait! Stop, Charie! Just listen. You're panicking. Help me, Holy Spirit,* I prayed.

Then he placed a book in my hands. The title glared at me: *Love and Respect.* This was my gift? Because my face is so transparent, I couldn't hide my emotions, so I chose not to speak right away. I'm sure I looked dumbfounded, but I finally smiled and thanked him.

Secretly, I was hoping he would leave so I could stop trying to conceal my disappointment. I needed a few minutes to process the situation, to regroup, to compose myself. I was anxious and slightly offended. But I knew he loved me and we had a good marriage. I didn't want to misinterpret his intentions, but the title felt threatening and accusing. I should have probably asked him a few questions to clarify his intentions, but I think I was afraid of his answer.

Clayton offered a reprieve: "I don't know if it's any good. We don't have to read it if you don't want to." I knew my face was filled with anxiety and disappointment. I was unsure if he was trying to give me a hint with the book, and I was also wondering why I wasn't holding chocolates instead. My voice probably sounded unsure, but I was able to respond, "No. It's okay. If they read it, it's probably really good."

My heart was conflicted over knowing my husband loved me and wondering if I hadn't met his expectations. I felt trapped by my emotions. How could a Christ-fearing wife of an evangelist tell her husband she's intimidated by a book entitled *Love and Respect?* Did he feel

I needed a little guidance in the area of respect? *Well,* I hoped, *maybe it'll be a little more about love than respect.*

Clayton offered to get the boys ready for bed and left the room. I was relieved.

After he left, I realized I hadn't paid attention to what he'd said because I'd been thinking too loudly, so I tried to remember. First, I'd heard the title. Second, the book had changed our friends' lives. And third, he wanted to read it together.

I was most afraid of number three. I decided I was willing to accept correction by myself, but I didn't know if I could read the book with him, because I didn't want to feel accused if some of my attitudes landed in the disrespectful category. I sat for about five minutes examining the cover.

I started crying, and after a few sobs, I picked up the book and began reading. The obvious question would be, "How did it go?" For the first few chapters I felt nailed to the wall. I was reading scriptures about husbands and wives that I had known for years, but the perspective was new and convicting. After a few chapters, I realized this wasn't the gift I had hoped for, but the one I needed. God had much to teach this defensive woman's heart before I was able to share what I learned with my well-intentioned husband.

Fears, Hopes, and Expectations

Dr. Eggerichs, the author of *Love and Respect,* hit a chord in my heart I hadn't known was hypersensitive. I'm used to hearing messages about how men are commanded to love their women, and that we're all commanded to love each other. But I'd never heard, or maybe just closed my ears, to the parts of Scripture that actually command a woman to respect her husband. When the author proposed this idea, I had to get out my Bible.

Is a woman really given the duty of respecting her husband? I had always thought respect was earned, a kind of reward for good behavior, but in the Scripture it is most definitely a command. This idea threatened me.

Some of you may also have this fear. Maybe you were tempted to skip this chapter because you're afraid you're going to hear that God designed women to be weak, mild, and timid, given the purpose of blindly submitting to men.

If this is true, does it mean God created a woman incomplete, incapable of living without a man—weak-willed, weak-minded? Is it biblical to say that women are meant to live lives of subjugation and suppression?

Maybe you're sick of people telling you that you're incomplete because you aren't married. Possibly you've been hurt by men in the past—and you were determined to prove you were fine without one. But now you're dating or engaged to the man you believe God has for you. And the transition from being alone and independent to sharing your life with this man makes you apprehensive.

Men, maybe you're scared of the idea of being "tied down." Maybe you wonder what it means to be a leader, the "head" of a family, because you haven't come from a family with a father you admired. You have no idea how a godly husband is supposed to interact with his wife. You hope she will respect you, but you are afraid she won't. And you don't know how to tell her you need her admiration. You want to be respected but are afraid to ask for it.

Perhaps you're hoping this chapter will encourage your independent woman to embrace a more yielding spirit with you. While you were dating or just engaged, her independence and spunk was complementary to your freedom. You appreciated the fact that she wasn't clingy and let you "hang with the guys." But now, you fear that her confidence and autonomy may hinder your ability to lead, to fulfill your role as a man. Perhaps the idea of loving her as you love yourself is intimidating because you don't "get" all her complexities.

Whatever your fears, hopes, or expectations, Clayton and I want to encourage you that we have no agenda in this chapter other than examining the Scriptures to find the heart of biblical submission. These concepts are not only essential to experience a healthy marriage, but also are useful in our relationships with other believers. We will look at the goodness God intended through His provision of submission. How the role of a woman and man in marriage is to honor one another. As God honors us through His interaction with us, so also we reflect Him in our service to one another.

Proverbs 2:1-2 gives a promise:

> *My child, never forget the things I have taught you.*
> *Store my commands in your heart.*
> *If you do this, you will live many years,*
> *and your life will be satisfying.*[1]

God wants us to live long, satisfied lives together, and we must never forget that. Just like I had to remember my husband's love for me when he gave me the book, we have to remember God loves us as we read the book He gave us.

DEFINITIONS

According the Merriam-Webster dictionary, *submission* comes from the Latin word *submittere*, which means "to lower." Below are a couple of definitions from Webster's:

1. the condition of being submissive, humble, or compliant
2. an act of submitting to the authority or control of another

---

What Is Submission?

We live in a world where one in four teenage girls will be raped or molested, and one in six boys will be abused. Bullying is increasing in schools, and sex trafficking, already epidemic, is increasing rapidly. In a culture filled with fear of domination, neglect, and abuse, many of us throw up our fists in opposition to any form of "submitting to the authority or control of another," or "being submissive, humble, or compliant" (see the definition above).

Our culture tells us to protect ourselves and elevate individual independence. We're never encouraged to serve someone else. We're taught if someone offers you help, there must be a catch. This is what our world teaches, but what does God's Word teach? What are His expectations of us as wives and husbands?

Understanding Paul

Mutual Submission

> Submit *to one another out of reverence for Christ. Wives,* submit *to your husbands as to the Lord. For the husband is the head of the wife as Christ is the head of the church, his body, of which he is the Savior. Now as the church* submits *to Christ, so also wives should* submit *to their husbands in everything. Husbands,* love *your wives, just as Christ* loved *the church and gave himself up for her...In the same way, husbands* ought *to* love *their wives as their own bodies. He who* loves *his wife* loves *himself...However, each one of you also must* love *his wife as he* loves *himself, and the wife must* respect *her husband.*[2]

This passage (and the surrounding chapters) shows us that there is no submission without love, and there is no love without submission. Paul, the writer of these commands, lived in a male-dominated society, and it was this cultural context Jesus was born into, and within which the early church lived out the good news Jesus brought in His resurrection.

Neither Romans, Greeks, nor Jews placed much value on women. They were considered little more than property. In Greek culture

> many men felt that women were morally weaker than men...Earlier philosophers were credited with a prayer of gratitude that they were not women. The moralist Plutarch allows that women can acquire virtues, and he praises the bravery of virtuous women throughout history. But when Plutarch argues that women should learn philosophy from their husbands, it is in part because he believes that if left to themselves, apart from men, women will produce only evil passions and foolishness.[3]

Similar to Plutarch (and who doesn't love Plutarch?), Jewish men also had some negative attitudes toward women.

> Jewish women were to be honored, but mistrust of women's moral character in Jewish texts is often stronger than what we find in the philosophers…An early Jewish teacher whose work was undoubtedly known to Paul advised men not to sit among women, because evil comes from them like a moth emerging from clothes. A man's evil, this teacher went on to complain, is better than a woman's good, for she brings only shame and reproach.[4]

For centuries, and across many cultures, women have been dominated by men who classify them in the same category with animals and property. Rome was also no exception. In his book *Paul, Women, and Wives,* Craig S. Keener describes the Roman social structure, in which women expected to be controlled and ruled by their husbands:

> Traditional Roman writers portrayed the feminine ideal as supportive and subservient. Roman inscriptions similarly indicate that women were usually honored for their roles as mothers, wives, or daughters, even though they sometimes made other contributions to society…This did not mean that a woman would never be valued or praised for her wisdom, but the most standard womanly ideal included a quiet and reclusive demeanor, and other elements were, for normal women, at best incidental.[5]

Countering the Culture

If you're a woman reading this, you probably want to go back in time and knock some sense into Romans, Greeks, and Jews alike. You may also be mad at Paul because you feel he is giving them more leverage for domination. But if we dig a bit deeper, we will be surprised to see that he is actually ascribing the woman her dignity and worth in Christ, thus elevating her to being an equal to the man.

Paul was an apostle and a leader in a world where Christians were the minority. Rome had the power to suppress and eliminate any religion, people group, or movement they felt was threatening to Caesar. Paul was not a political figure. He was an evangelist and teacher, serving and encouraging suppressed believers. He had to be wise in the way he taught the congregations of believers.

When considering Ephesians 5, understand that it wouldn't have been offensive for a woman of Paul's time to hear that she should be submissive. In fact, public teaching often told husbands how to keep their wives obedient. Paul's command to respect or submit was not intended to demean the woman. Instead, his words would have caused a man to react with offense!

Why? Keener points out,

> Paul is certainly among the minority of ancient writers in that he devotes more space to the exhortation of husbands to love in Ephesians 5 than to that of the wives to submit. In our culture, his exhortation to wives to submit stands out more strongly; in his culture, the exhortation to husbands to love rather than the normal advice to rule the home, would have stood out more strongly. Further, Paul does not address the husband's role in the wife's submission; he does not urge the husband to inculcate submission in his wife. Paul's only instructions to the husband are to serve her as Christ served the church, and since husband and wife are "one flesh," to love her as he would his own body. Paul does not call on wives to take charge of their husbands, but calls on husbands to love their wives in such a radical way that husbands become their wives servants too.[6]

Paul is careful not to aggressively attack the guidelines of the Roman political-social structure because this tactic would have brought the weight of the empire crashing down on the early church. Instead, the Spirit inspires him to be as wise as a serpent, but as innocent as a dove. The apostle encourages women to remain faithful in their submission, but he shocks his male audience by asking them to lay down their lives for their wives. This was countercultural (as it still is in the twenty-first century), but the concept of mutual submission, with the husband as the loving leader, was consistent with the gospel, originating from the example of Jesus.

Why Should We Submit?

To Imitate Christ

The call for wives to submit to their husbands is written in partnership with the call for Christians to submit to one another out of reverence for Christ.

What does practical submission look like for a wife? Wives are encouraged to humble their wills to their husbands not because men are more significant or worthy, but out of respect and in honor of Jesus. If Christ was able to suffer humiliation and death for the ultimate good of humanity, He will also give us the desire and capability to serve our husbands in the same manner. The paraphrase from *The Message* says it beautifully: "A wife should put her husband first as she does the Lord." Read also the New International Reader's Version: "Wives, follow the lead of your husbands as you follow the Lord." We are asked to submit to our husbands, first because Christ set this example for us as believers, but also because the person you are married to is a child of God. God is calling you to imitate His love for your husband in your respect and submission toward him as the head of the home.

Paul's command in verse 21 to "submit to one another out of reverence for Christ" was directed to men as well as women. In verses 25-33, he instructs husbands to love their wives, "just as Christ loved the church and gave himself up for her," which can be seen as an ultimate act of submission through death.

The point is that we are all to "be imitators of God, as dearly loved children. And walk in love, as the Messiah also loved us and gave Himself for us, a sacrificial and fragrant offering to God."[7] This verse indicates that since we are children of God, we are called to imitate Christ's behavior. He had an attitude of humility, laying down His life for us on the cross. We should follow suit.

To Emanate Christ

The call to submit is a call to show people what the love of God is really like. It is a high calling, not an embarrassment. Women, God is not calling you to submit because your husbands are genetically superior. Men, God is not calling you to give your lives for your wives because He wants you to be nothing but workhorses. We are supposed to "live a life filled with love, following the example of Christ. He loved us and offered himself as a sacrifice for us, a pleasing aroma to God."[8] How was Jesus' sacrifice a fragrant offering to God? It was because His death gave us life and took away God's wrath against our sin.

When we submit to one another in our marriages, they begin to smell sweeter to the world around us. We become a fragrant offering as people see our willingness to love each other more than ourselves. In this way, marriage also becomes an opportunity to show people the gospel, the only way to life.

We've all seen married couples who exude frustration. They fight. They roll their eyes. They speak to each other with condescension. They make the room tense and uncomfortable. The crowd musters their happy faces…someone tries to offer a distraction…but secretly everyone wishes the pair would go somewhere else and work it out. This is the couple nobody wants to be around.

You've also seen the couple who can't get enough of each other. They *love* to be around each other, and everyone loves to be around them. Sure, they also experience moments of frustration, but overall they respect one another. They laugh, speak with tenderness, and they enjoy each other. You may be jealous of them at times because that's the kind of marriage we all want.

Each of these marriages emanates its own aroma. One makes you want to close your eyes, wrinkle your nose, and cringe, and the other makes you want to watch with curiosity and stay to enjoy the perfume. You might wonder what makes them work so well together.

Understanding Peter

Speaking of working together, did you know that when God looked on Adam He determined that the first man had no suitable helper?

And so He created a woman. Genesis 1:26-28 says that mankind (man and woman) was created first to embody the image of God, but also to have "dominion" over everything in the ocean, in the air, and on the earth. Together, they were called to "subdue" and to be fruitful. Adam could not do this alone, so God brings him a "helper."

Now pay attention, because this is important. The Hebrew word for "helper" is *ezer,* meaning "strong helper." This word "is used most often (sixteen of twenty-one occurrences) in the Old Testament to refer to God as Israel's helper in times of trouble."[9] The connotation of *ezer* makes it comparable to the word *warrior.*

What Does "Weaker" Mean?

Why do I bring this up? Because I have been approached by countless confused females who wonder what God is saying in the book of 1 Peter, chapter 3.

At the end of chapter 2, Peter points first to the example of Christ, just as Paul did:

> Christ suffered for you, leaving you an example, that you should follow in his steps. "He committed no sin, and no deceit was found in his mouth." When they hurled their insults at him, he did not retaliate; when he suffered, he made no threats. Instead, he entrusted himself to him who judges justly.[10]

After two more verses that describe Christ's work to save us, then comes the difficult part:

> Wives, in the same way be submissive to your husbands so that, if any of them do not believe the word, they may be won over without words by the behavior of their wives, when they see the purity and reverence of your lives. Your beauty should not come from outward adornment, such as braided hair and the wearing of gold jewelry and fine clothes. Instead, it should be that of your inner self, the unfading beauty of a gentle and quiet spirit, which is of great worth in God's sight. For this is the way the holy

women of the past who put their hope in God used to make themselves beautiful...

Husbands, in the same way be considerate as you live with your wives, and treat them with respect as the weaker partner and as heirs with you of the gracious gift of life, so that nothing will hinder your prayers. [11]

Just what is God asking ask of wives, of women? The Scripture specifically encourages them to submit, to let their beauty be expressed by internal values rather than external adorning, to adopt a gentle and quiet spirit, and it instructs men to honor them as a "weaker vessel" (ESV). What does this mean? If women were also created in the image of God to be a strong helper, why are they described as the "weaker partner"?

To begin, Peter and Paul's teachings about submission correspond. Submission is relationally beneficial, it is a calling for any believer, and it is also indispensable so that we reflect the power of Christ's service to us.

Inner beauty and submission. Peter's emphasis on beauty would have brought to his hearers' minds the traditions of the aristocratic class in Rome. Throughout history, many cultures have worshipped the human form and earthly pleasure. Our culture is no exception, nor was Roman society. Men would lavishly adorn their wives as a competition. Who had the bigger trophy? (Does this seem a little familiar?) This created pressure among women in the church to obsess over their appearance, or feel compelled to outdo each other with lavish accessories. In comparison, Peter reminds us how the "holy women who hoped in God used to adorn themselves" (verse 5 ESV). What is the legacy of the women who are esteemed in Scripture? Are they admired for what they wore—or for who they were, how they lived, and how they loved their husbands?

Honor and consideration. Next, Peter commands husbands to "live with your wives in an understanding way, showing honor to the woman as the weaker vessel, since they are heirs with you of the grace of life, so that your prayers may not be hindered" (verse 7 ESV). In the same way as many cultures before or since, the society of Peter's time "argued that women were by nature inferior to men in every way except sexually."[12] Husbands were justified in taking advantage of their wives' lesser physical strength to control, intimidate, and overpower them, and even beat them into subjugation if deemed necessary. This treatment of wives continues to be common today, though our society calls it "abuse" and does not try to justify it.

However, Peter teaches that a wife is redeemed by the same grace as her husband. They are equally heirs of God's gift of life. Husbands are therefore to honor them and treat them with consideration. If the men are faithful in this, their prayers will not be hindered.

Submission vs. Control

The key is submission.

When we received Christ, we became one with Him. In order to understand submission, we have to begin by knowing that God was our first example. Why were you drawn to Christ? Was it because He was willing to love you to the point of death? This is how He captured my heart. The very act of giving up your autonomy and independence requires submission. Just as we want to know and serve Christ, we should also want to know and serve each other so that our marriage becomes a testimony to the world of God's grace in Christ...in that we were willing to literally submit by sacrificing our identity as a single person and taking a new identity with our husband or wife as a couple, as one flesh. This is true love, true submission.

Subjugation Doesn't Foster Love

There is a vast difference between a healthy submissive relationship and one of domination and control. Because abuse toward children and women has become so common, it is imperative to distinguish between submission and subjugation. We must not only discern the difference, but also become sensitive to the pain the abused may have experienced.

I knew a woman who was taken advantage of physically when she was of grade-school age. When she inherited a stepfather through marriage, this girl was too young to remember living with her father. Therefore, she didn't know it was perverse for the stepfather to invite her into his bed for physical intimacy. After a few years, her eyes were opened to his secret exploitation. Shame invaded her heart. She felt different and alone. Now conscious that this was something only a husband and wife were supposed to share, she feared her mother's hurt and possible anger.

This woman felt ostracized and different from her friends, and constantly wondered if people could see the indignity, hurt, and embarrassment in her eyes. Could they see the dark secrets in her soul? Would she ever feel normal again? Her stepdad seldom spoke to her. He rarely engaged in her life except when it was time for physical manipulation. She was forced into "loving" this man. She was coerced, used to satisfy a perverted lust. This abuse planted seeds of shame, mistrust, and isolation in her.

This girl's story is one of countless such abuses throughout history. Even today, women, girls, and boys are being bought and sold as slaves in the sex industry. Once they've been exploited, they often don't have the strength to leave what they've known. Many times they are raped into subjugation, so they feel degraded and hopeless—trapped and abandoned with no hope for love or rescue. The painful domination they are forced into has become a breeding ground for insecurity, anger, and bitterness. As a result, sadly, the good word *submission* has become associated with such sinful practices.

Although a Christian may affirm a clear biblical understanding of God's absolute sovereign rule, we still struggle to understand His divine design in tragedy and loss. Yet we know He loves us. And the thing that gets us through our most difficult times is often not answers to our questions, but the relationship of intimacy itself. Godly relationship is the foundation, the reason a wife can learn to support and stand beside her man. It is also the motivation a husband needs in order to lead in love rather than through manipulation and control. God doesn't kick down the door of our hearts, forcing His way in. He knocks, whispers, and waits. Life with Him, like marriage, is a chosen opportunity, not a forced obligation.

We relate to God in submission fueled by love and intimacy, not by fear or a blind adherence to cold principles. You were not created to have a slave relationship with the Most High, and neither are you to be a slave to your spouse. This is the foundation of submission. We offer our lives freely to God in response to His grace, and He completes us. This should also be the foundational principle for submission in marriage. Are you willing to submit like this?

The Ultimate Example of Humble Submission

God Himself is the ultimate example of loving submission because it characterizes the life of the Trinity.

Each Person of the Trinity deserves glory as God and is justified in receiving it. However, they choose to humble themselves one to another. This eternal circle of splendor, of deferring to the other, encapsulates the true, essential character of our unselfish, all-powerful God. He is altogether incapable of abusive love or repression.

He is three Persons in one being. We also become one in marriage. When we unite, we become one in a way that points to the oneness of God. We leave our families to become part of another. If we follow God's example, we are two people seeking to serve each other, and if we do this right we also glorify Him in the process. We become part of the circle of submission.

*

Does submission seem so horrendous to you now? Mark Driscoll, pastor at Mars Hill Church in Seattle, once said that when you become more concerned with *service* than *self* in your marriage, that's when it really gets sweet. He said this usually occurs when you've been married between 9 and 14 years. So when it gets tough early on, remember the sweet years are coming. Clayton and I have been married since 1999 and we can truly say it is sweet. I'm still learning to serve (and so is Clayton), but much of my selfishness has waned, by God's grace. And I'm not afraid of submission anymore, either.

I could tell you how I submit to Clayton, but we are all different.

It's important for you to discuss what submission looks like practically for each of you. As you finish the chapter, think about these questions:

1. Is there anything in your past you need to talk about that would make it hard to submit?

2. Have you ever thought about submission as a good and godly virtue that breeds love and intimacy?

3. Is there a pride issue in your heart that makes you cringe at the thought of submitting to another person?

4. If God submits in humility in the Trinity and humbles Himself as a servant of humanity, what does that say about our willingness to submit and serve?

5. What makes you feel served and respected?

6. Are there any attitudes that need to be refined so your future testimony as a couple reflects the gospel?

Chapter 10

Will You Give Respect?

She was my pleasing companion, my most affectionate friend,
my judicious counselor. I seldom, if ever, repented of acting
according to her advice. And I seldom, if ever, acted against
it without being convinced by the event that I was wrong.

JOHN NEWTON'S WORDS ABOUT HIS WIFE, POLLY.
NEWTON, A FORMER SLAVE SHIP CAPTAIN, BECAME A
CHRISTIAN LEADER AND WROTE THE HYMN "AMAZING GRACE."
WILLIAM PETERSON, FROM *25 SURPRISING MARRIAGES*

Our first couple years of marriage, Clayton and I traveled together full-time. He often introduced me from stage, saying what a wonderful woman he had married, how lucky he was, how great I was, and so on. People probably wished they had someone to brag on them like that, but I always saw it as a way for Clayton to break the ice, a way to entertain the audience. He was communicating love to me in "his language"—and I was missing it.

We would return home and I'd wash the clothes, fold them, and pack his bag neatly. I was loving him in "my language," but he just felt like I was doing what needed to be done to get on the road. We were showing love to one another, but in our own ways—and neither of us was seeing the other's love.

A few years and a few children later, I finally started to notice how consistent Clayton's pleas for verbal encouragement had become. But I reasoned it away. I saw him as a confident person, and besides, other people were always encouraging him. At each event, I watched as students, parents, and youth pastors showered him with compliments. After these, it seemed like mine would be inconsequential. When I would share this with Clayton, his response was always, "Yes, but you are my wife and I *need* your encouragement. I don't *need* theirs. I *need* you, Charie." He tried to explain how much he valued my admiration and approval, but I didn't feel prestigious enough to make a difference.

It didn't matter how many times he reassured me, I was unable to embrace the concept. I was intimidated by verbal affirmation because we didn't really do this much in our home growing up, and because I think I was scared to sound foolish. My pride was trapping me. And finally, since I'm confessing, you should know I kind of resented the fact that he often received praise from everyone while I sat in the shadows. Yep. I think my pride was the main obstacle.

My stubbornness didn't make sense, but I simply refused to humble myself. I avoided giving him what he needed. Instead I worked more around the house and even started to point out everything I was doing for him. I bet you can guess that my increased servitude and guilt-provoking comments didn't change Clayton's emotional makeup. He still needed the same thing—my verbal approval.

Loving someone can be tricky because our motives for love are sometimes unclear. Did I truly want to serve and love my husband, or was I really serving myself by looking for appreciation? It was probably a little of both, but if I wasn't willing to love him in the way he needed, I was really only pleasing myself.

She had one abiding purpose: to show him she loved him, and she peeled away the layers of pride one by one until she was humbled by her own nakedness…She thought she had been saved by his love for her, and in part she had been. It cleansed her, never casting blame. But that had only been the beginning. It was loving him in return that brought her up out of the darkness.[1]

—FRANCINE RIVERS, FROM *REDEEMING LOVE*

Will You Make the Choice?

The passage above from the book *Redeeming Love* describes what took place in my heart toward my husband. I remember the day my heart truly embraced his need for respect.

I was reading the book *For Women Only* by Shaunti Feldhahn and ran across these words. "While it may be totally foreign to most of us, the male need for respect and affirmation—especially from his woman—is so hard wired and so critical that most men would rather feel unloved than disrespected or inadequate." The survey indicated that if they had to choose one of the following two situations, 74 percent of men would rather be alone and unloved than feel inadequate and be disrespected. Only 26 percent chose the other way around. Shaunti comments,

> Finally the lightbulb came on: If a man feels disrespected, he is going to feel unloved. And what that translates to is this: If you want to love your man in the way he needs to be loved, then you need to ensure that he feels your respect most of all. [2]

The minute I read this, I saw just how blind I had been. I was letting other people love Clayton the way he needed to be loved while I watched, all because I was afraid to sound ignorant and insignificant. So I looked at my choices: Hide behind my pride and ignore my husband's feelings, or believe him and hope to make a difference.

In her book *Satisfy My Thirsty Soul*, Linda Dillow shares,

> One night when I couldn't sleep, I looked up the word encourage. The root word is courage. The prefix en means "to put into," so when I tell my husband how much I respect him for responding with love to someone who hurt him, I put courage into him. What a great thought! I also looked up the prefix dis. It means "to separate from." So when I speak discouraging words to my husband I separate him from the courage he needs to be a godly man. Not such a great thought.
>
> If encouragement does not easily flow from your lips, it

might feel as if you're speaking a foreign language when you begin to use words to build up others. But persevere, because words of encouragement give fresh energy to your children and also to your friends.[3]

Linda's words reminded me of myself. I needed to know that I could put courage into Clayton. It's not that I was negative, nagging, or oppressive—I was simply withholding love by not giving respect. But if you think about it, if I wasn't "putting in" to him, I was actually separating him from something he needed. Something he had asked for, not once, but many times. I tried to reason that he didn't need it, but he wouldn't give up—thankfully.

My Choice...and What Followed

The Roman emperor Marcus Aurelius is reported to have said, "Because a thing seems difficult for you, do not think it impossible." Taking Marcus Aurelius' and Linda Dillow's advice, I decided to take the plunge. I would nurture and cultivate Clayton's confidence. I would express my undying devotion to and delight in him. I would tell him how wonderful I thought he was and how much I loved him. I'd been hesitant too long. Now I would take action and respect his need to hear my words of affirmation.

I wish I could tell you God miraculously intervened and poetic words of eloquence and power fell from my lips. It was quite the opposite. After an event, we were finally alone in the car. Pumped up on adrenaline, I nervously I blurted out, "You did a *great* job. I really thought the scriptures and illustrations were *neat*. That was really *great* and I felt like everyone thought you were *neat*." (I won't be offended if you laugh at me right now.)

Silence followed, and I thought, *Where's a thesaurus when you need it? "Great" and "neat"?* Nervous sweat began to drip down my back, and my face turned red. My hands were clasped and felt clammy. I couldn't look Clayton in the eye because I was so embarrassed. I looked down to the floor mats. Why was this so hard for me? Then he turned to offer me a grin. I think my blunder had surprised us both and we relieved the tension with laughter. He took my hand, looked into my hesitant eyes, and thanked me. We held hands for a long time. If Clayton's dry soul could have spoken, it would have gushed a delightful "ahhh." In this moment I was convinced that humbling yourself for someone you adore strengthens you both. It truly is better to give than receive.

I continued to feel ridiculous each time I affirmed Clayton, but each effort became easier because he knew I was trying. He heard my heart and not just my words, and he'd try to help me. If I was complimenting him and stopped, he would ask more questions in a show of mock arrogance. Like, when I'd say he was the best husband ever, he'd say, "How do you know? 'Cause you can't even pay attention to anyone else when you've got such a magnificent specimen of a husband right here in front of you." I'd laugh and continue, disarmed. He was grasping more and more just how much I respected and loved him.

I had always felt it, but didn't know how much hearing it encouraged him, and how much not hearing it caused him to question my feelings. Sophistication is overrated. When we take ourselves too seriously, we miss the opportunity to grow and to help and encourage each other. Giving respect benefits the relationship, not just the individual.

And guys, remember this: "Most women really do feel great respect and appreciation for their husband or boyfriend but don't always know how to show it. In fact ninety-three percent of women may not always show it well, but actually deeply need, respect and desire their husband or significant other."[4]

Why Do We Give Respect?

...Because We Are His Creation

So many times we miss opportunities to honor each other. Maybe we're missing this call because we're forgetting where we've come from. Why should we respect one another? Because of who we are in Christ! We are children of God—redeemed by Him. Each one of us carries worth because we are loved by our Savior. Why did God value our lives enough to save us? Because we are His creation, made in His likeness. We respect each other first because of where we've come from. We came from God.

I'm an oil painter, and hope soon to experiment with acrylics also. My works are an expression of me. Often what I paint is an outward expression of what the Lord is doing in my heart. If I were to share a painting with someone and they took out a knife and began slashing the canvas, I would be heartbroken and angry! In the same way, people are a display of God's work of creativity: "We are God's masterpiece. He has created us anew in Christ Jesus so we can do good things he planned for us long ago."[5]

We treat one another with honor because He created our inmost being; He knit us together in our mother's womb. We praise Him because we are fearfully and wonderfully made; His works are wonderful, we know that full well.[6] Why are we called to respect each other? Because each of us is fearfully and wonderfully made! Your mate is God's creation, whether man or woman, he or she needs to feel important and valued. God placed tremendous value on your mate and planned good things for them long ago.[7] He has a plan and purpose for them, and when you affirm them, they are better equipped to fulfill that purpose. You are worshiping Him by honoring the person He created. You get to share life with a creation of God. Do you know that "full well"?

Honor isn't passive, it's active...Honor not expressed is not honor.[8]

—GARY AND BETSY RICUCCI, FROM *LOVE THAT LASTS*

...Because We Are Instructed To

As is the case with submission, we are in touchy territory when we talk about giving respect. As we enter this section, which discusses the Bible's commands, please remember a few things. First, we've already learned about the purpose of submission. Next, remember the story I shared at the beginning of this chapter and know that I'm not perfect. Then, please let the Word of God speak to your heart, not just to your intellect or to past offenses. And finally, take a moment to pray for receptive ears.

Okay, so we're traveling back to the idea that a woman is instructed to respect her husband. When I was reading Ephesians 5, I came to the part that said "a wife must respect her husband." When I got here, I was really tempted to skip the word *must*. Actually, skipping the entire phrase wouldn't have been difficult, because it's at the end of the chapter. However, the Holy Spirit wouldn't let me. I asked myself why I wanted to skip this verse. I have a feeling it's because most of us have offenses from the past. So first we have to deal with the past in order to find the respect our husbands deserve. (This is not for women only. Husbands must also respect their wives. But it's more difficult for the woman, which may be why Paul *specifically* instructs *wives* to give respect and husbands to give love.)

Detecting offenses. Nearly all of us have offenses from our past that have affected us to some degree. As a woman, I know how difficult it is for us to overcome them, especially in a world that often demeans, devalues, and takes advantage of women. It's so hard for us to respect our husbands partly because of our own issues and partly because of how women are treated worldwide. According to Nicholas Kristof and Sheryl WuDunn,

> About 107 million females are missing from the globe today…Every year, at least another 2 million girls worldwide disappear because of gender discrimination…The global statistics on the abuse of girls are numbing. It appears that more girls have been killed in the last fifty years, precisely because they were girls, than men were killed in all the battles of the twentieth century. More girls are killed in this routine "gendercide" in any one decade than people were slaughtered in all the genocides of the twentieth century.
>
> In America, millions of women and girls face beatings or other violence from their husbands or boyfriends, and more than one in six undergoes rape or attempted rape at some point in her life, according to the National Violence Against Women survey. Then there is forced prostitution. Teenage runaways are beaten, threatened, and branded (with tattoos) by pimps in American cities, and thousands of foreign women are trafficked into the United States as well.[9]

Can you believe this? No wonder we have such negative gut reactions when we hear that God commands women to respect their husbands. Millions of women grow up as victims of abuse, and then they're expected to conjure up feelings of trust and appreciation as they enter marriage? You see how hard this can be.

The truth is, many of us need healing, but we don't know we're hurting because the rest of the world is hurting as well. A voice inside us says, *Stay strong. Don't give respect unless it's earned or you'll be the next victim.*

This perspective is understandable, but it will poison a marriage. If your husband is holy and dearly loved by God, doesn't he deserve your respect based on his God-given intrinsic worth?

Mistrust from our past affects our present. If we remain victims of the past, we make our husband one as well. He is not the one who hurt you, so you can't treat him as such. He is not your abuser—he is your lover, your life partner. If you are going to honor his position, you have to let go of the hurt from past offenses. (Please understand that I'm not advocating that you stay in an abusive or destructive relationship. If you are in such a relationship, you have God-given permission to protect yourself. Get out and get help.)

Why is it so hard to let go of past hurts? Sometimes we are like an animal that gets its foot caught in a trap. It lies there in agony. At first it may squirm or try to get loose. But as the pain increases, the creature's efforts to free itself hurt too much. If anyone tries to free it, it is in so much pain it may attack its liberator. Other animals refuse to stay in a trap. They will gnaw their leg off before they endure one more second in agony. A hurting animal will hurt you if you try to rescue it from a trap. In the same way, *hurting people hurt people.*

Our souls are trapped within our misery. Our wounds become so familiar, we can't see that brokenness is our liberator. Somehow, we think if we just stay strong, we will be better off. Brokenness and healing become our enemy, and sooner or later we look inside to find a trap clutching our souls. Gradually we become so familiar with *who we are* that we can't see *who we could become.* Bitterness makes God's command to respect each other seem inhumane and unjust.

Letting go of offenses. Respect is not a door to oppression, however. The Lord wants you to experience freedom, liberty, and healing. But He also wants this for your mate. If you don't let the Lord heal your unresolved wounds, you're not only keeping yourself in slavery, but you're pulling your spouse along with you.

The two of you are becoming one, so *who you are is also who he will become*. It is a great mystery how we become one with each other. Have you ever noticed people start to look alike when they've been married awhile? Well, people start acting alike too. If you let unresolved unforgiveness and hurt from a previous situation keep you from honoring your man, he will eventually start withholding love from you. Maybe not purposefully or intentionally, but he will feel your lack of admiration and this will affect your relationship.

I have written most of this section to women, but I am not ignorant of the fact that men are victims of abuse as well. The principles above are also applicable to guys. The situations may be different, but it's important for a man to heal from his past in order to treat his wife with the care and honor she deserves. If you've been violently abused by a father, you need to forgive so you can come to the realization that your wife is not your enemy and does not deserve to be the victim of your outbursts. Just as you want to be honored and respected, so does she.

So, men and women, I cannot diagnose your hearts. But please let the Lord search your soul, "since he knows the secrets of the heart."[10] Lewis Smedes encouraged me with this quote: "As we start on the miracle of forgiving, we begin to see our enemy through a cleaner lens, less smudged by hate. A person who shares our faulty humanity, bruised like us, faulty like us, still thoroughly blamable for what he did to us. Yet human like us."[11] When our hearts open themselves to brokenness, God removes us from the trap, forgiveness is initiated, and our wounds begin to heal.

...Because We Need It

We are not called to live like the world. We are different, so we have to fight the messages it sends us. One of the world's prevailing lies is that we don't need to honor and respect someone unless they are earning it.

Unless they're up to par. Unless they're pulling their weight. But do we really think that by withholding respect, they will be properly motivated to step up their game? This is manipulation, and manipulation never leads to love and respect. Do you admire those who manipulate you?

God wants us to respect each other even when we don't act in a way deserving of respect. The strange irony is that by giving honor and respect to our spouse when they are not acting honorably, we actually can change their heart and their behavior.

Goethe said, "Treat a man as he is, and he will remain as he is. Treat a man as he can and should be, and he will become what he can and should be."[12] When we degrade another person, they absorb the attitude we send their way. Eventually, they come to believe they are the way we treat them. However, if we motivate them by emphasizing their strengths, they will grow.

The story at the beginning of this chapter is a prime example. Clayton was becoming increasingly discouraged. I could see it on his face when he came home. But by verbally affirming him, I gave him an opportunity to grow as a man and a person. We can either be a part of our lover's growth, or we can sit on the sidelines offering criticism when they don't meet our every expectation.

In Colossians 3, Paul gives us a list of rules for holy living. Verses 18 and 19 address wives and husbands, so I'd like add a summary of what the verses leading up to these say because I think they tell us a little more practically how to respect one another:

> As God's chosen people, be kind and have compassion. Be humble, gentle and have patience with each other. Forgive each other. Why? Because God forgave you. Respect each other. Why? Because God made us. Strive for unity and peace in your marriage. Be thankful for the spouse God has given you, for their life and partnership. Encourage each other with scriptures, and share what God is doing in your own life. Share your joy and pains so that you can lift each other up with testimonies or worship songs.
>
> As you're living life together, wives, submit to your husband

instead of throwing his mistakes up in his face. And husbands, love your wives when you're disappointed or frustrated, instead of reacting with anger or violence. This is how we respect each other.[13]

When a woman knows her husband values her opinion, her wants, her feelings, her desires, and even her idiosyncrasies, she doesn't care as much about the rest of the world's opinion of her. If he's made her feel like she's the most important woman on earth, she can let the lies of the world roll off her back. I know because my husband does this for me.

When a man knows his wife's got his back, he's motivated to conquer the world. Mark Driscoll says that a man's home is his woman. A woman's home is most often the house, but a man finds home wherever his wife is. When a woman honors her man, his heart is strengthened because he's found a secure and trustworthy home. When the world is against him, she's his place of rest and safety. This is why she needs to esteem him above all other men.

Ultimately, we human beings, whether we realize it or not, are involved in a cosmic spiritual conflict that pits God against Satan, with marriage and the family serving as a key arena in which spiritual and cultural battles are fought. If, then, the cultural crisis is symptomatic of an underlying spiritual crisis, the solution likewise must be spiritual, not merely cultural.[14]

—ANDREAS KÖSTENBERGER, FROM *GOD, MARRIAGE AND FAMILY*

...In Order to Be a Light

The significance of marriage is changing in our world. Whether you know it or not, the world is watching you. The debate as to whether Christianity, or any religion for that matter, keeps married people in love for life is a hot topic. Research is constantly being done on marriage. Is it still relevant? Should we even make the effort? Why not cohabit since it seems cheaper? What's the big deal anyway?

The modern world is turning its back on this holy institution, so we have the opportunity to offer the world a reason to believe in marriage. Outsiders often think Christians view marriage as a male-dominated institution where the woman is subjected to the will of a man simply because God thinks men are better. Of course this is untrue, but it serves as a reminder of how important it is for us to respect each other as a testimony to the value God places on both partners.

When you model mutual submission and respect in a world plagued by skepticism, cynicism, and abuse, your marriage will stand out. When the world sees your love for each other, it will wonder why you are different. By treating one another as highly valued children of God, you proclaim the gospel. Your marriage is an outreach. Live your marriage glorifying God, and He will produce good fruit through it. "Commit your works to the Lord and your plans will be established."[15]

People are attracted to those who admire them and
repelled by those who belittle or look down on them.[16]

—GARY SMALLEY, FROM *LOVING EACH OTHER FOR BETTER AND FOR BEST*

Practically Speaking

If you want your man to love you the way you need to be loved, then prepare yourself to respect him the way he needs to be respected. He will be attracted to you when you admire him.

Now that we've addressed the heart of this biblical directive, Clayton and I want to get practical. Realistically, the ways you show respect to your significant other are as diverse and complex as the person you marry. No one person has the same personality, thoughts, emotions, or background. But each person should be able to tell you what he or she needs. The goal is to make sure your spouse feels loved and respected, not controlled. You want to provide them a place of refuge, not captivity.

In Colossians 3 we saw qualities that will foster respect in your marriage: compassion, kindness, humility, gentleness, patience, forgiveness, love, thankfulness, peace, and unity. We were told to speak encouragement to one another. Below is a more hands-on list of ways you can make sure you're living out these principles. Discuss these and rate them in order of importance to you. Then tell each other how to specifically fulfill your needs. You may want to keep this list on hand because some areas may improve or need work with time. Then you can re-evaluate.

How to Begin Expressing Admiration for Each Other

1. Communicate often. Never close each other out.
2. Ask each other's opinions frequently and value them.
3. Seek each other's advice about decisions.
4. Be teachable without putting up your defenses.
5. Show your spouse more attention than you do other people.
6. Each of you brag about the other to people behind the other's back.
7. Defend each other to others; avoid criticism.
8. Be forgiving when they offend you.
9. Show your spouse you need them.
10. Tell your mate you're proud of them.
11. Help each other fulfill your dreams or callings.
12. Support each other's work, whether in the office or home.
13. Keep a list of things your spouse "hasn't gotten to" and help make them happen.
14. Develop a positive and gentle attitude with your spouse.
15. Remember that honor is active, not passive. Specifically find a way to honor your spouse each day.

God will give you the grace to respect your spouse if you are willing to ask Him. Don't wait until you think they deserve it. Prepare yourself now, before you're married, to give the honor and respect your mate will need. You will be amazed at how giving respect will begin transforming the one you love from the inside out. It will turn them into the kind of partner you've always dreamed of having, and it will make you a more humble, loving child of God.

Are you ready to respect?

Chapter 11

Are You Ready to Love?

ABOUT WILLIAM AND CATHERINE BOOTH,
FOUNDERS OF THE SALVATION ARMY:

*When you put together two determined people like
William and Catherine, both of who came from
problem marriages, you wouldn't expect to find the love
and commitment that was evidenced by the Booths.
They needed each other. At times they admonished
one another; at other times, they propped each other
up. The fact of the matter is they loved each other.*

WILLIAM PETERSON, FROM *25 SURPRISING MARRIAGES*

've got a love story for you. It's one you think Hollywood might script, only it's about two people who were in love with God first and ended up in love with each other. My brother, Chase, and his wife-to-be, Elisabeth, spent quite a lot of time hanging out with other friends at the beginning of their relationship. Chase was always secretive about his romantic feelings. He rarely talked to anyone because at age 28 he still hadn't dated anyone, so he got sick of the constant interrogations: *Who are you dating? When are you going to meet someone? Oooh! Do you like her? Are you going to marry her?*

His secretiveness also played into his relationship with Elisabeth. He would drop by her work and leave gifts, movie tickets, food, and other small items. She was trying to figure out if he was pursuing her or if he was just being kind and considerate. This is a common theme in young love: A guy enjoys a girl, the girl enjoys the guy. She is wondering what might come, and he's just having fun.

A little flirting developed into a relationship. With this being his first relationship ever, Chase kept things low-key. I think he was afraid it might escalate faster than he wanted if our family found out—and he wanted some space. They'd been dating for a while, and then I got a call from my frantic brother. He was worried Elisabeth was more in love with him than he her. I tried to assure him this was normal, that his feelings probably needed a little longer to surface, but he disagreed, and I gave up. He was scared to bring her closer. He didn't want to hurt her. So I assured him it would be better for him to let her go than lead her on.

A little later, after Chase's heart had been broken by a different girl, I got another emotional phone call. He confessed what a fool he'd been. He realized Elisabeth was perfect for him, and he wondered how he could let such a sincere and faithful love slip through his fingers. My heart sank. "Well," I said, "if you feel like that, you've got to try to win her back." He assured me it would never work. "She's a strong woman and I've hurt her. She'll never take me back. I hurt her too badly." I told him, "Well, you can't know if you don't try. It will be hard, but if she sees your humble heart, she might be able to forgive you. If she's that great you have to try."

A few months passed, and I didn't hear anything about the two of them. Then I got a call. "Do you have any frequent flyer miles saved up? I want to take Elisabeth to New York next week to ask her to marry me." Wow, this was a surprise! It had worked! I was so proud of his and Elisabeth's courage.

The New York trip didn't work out because it was too expensive and there was too little time to plan it. But Chase and Elisabeth were soon engaged, and they married on May 2, 2009. They live life together every day now.

What is marriage like for them? They're working every day toward a fulfilling and joyful relationship. Times have been hard. The recession kept my brother from finding a job for a long time, so he kept their daughter at home. He battled the discouragement of unemployment. Elisabeth is working full-time as an esthetician. She encourages her husband, and in turn she finds encouragement in his faithfulness and their beautiful little girl, Ruby Claire.

Love cleanses, beloved. It doesn't beat you down. It doesn't cast blame...My love isn't a weapon. It's a lifeline. Reach out and take hold, and don't let go.[1]

—FRANCINE RIVERS, FROM *REDEEMING LOVE*

Love Offers Safety

Why do I tell you Chase and Elisabeth's story? Well, first because it's just amazing. But also because there's a powerful message of what it means for a husband to give his life for his wife as Christ gave His life for the church. We're going to look back at Ephesians chapter 5 again. Verse 25 says that Christ "loved the church and gave himself up for her." He gave His life to win us. If you are a Christian, at some point you decided you wanted to rely on Jesus as your Savior. But before you made this decision, you had to decide that He was safe enough to give your life to. Maybe you had a certain moment with Him where you realized this. Maybe it was a process during which you learned He truly loved you and valued you enough to give His life for you.

Whatever the process, He proved Himself worthy of your trust. Men, this is what the Lord wants you to develop with your woman. She needs to feel you are a guy who believes she is worth winning and worth giving your life to. She has to believe you're safe, that you're going to protect her.

When my brother realized what a wonderful love he had lost in Elisabeth, he set out to win her back. I'm sure you women understand how devastating the breakup felt to Elisabeth. The feeling that you loved a guy more than he loved you is not exactly a safe feeling. So when Chase came back to her door, he had to work twice as hard to prove to her that maybe he hadn't appreciated her love in the past, but he wasn't going to make that mistake again. He was going to humble himself until she finally opened the door again.

Chase's walk back to love was probably filled with guilt, shame, and regret. Elisabeth was probably filled with anger, hurt, frustration, and hesitation. But it was his job to prove he was safe. It was his job to win her. It was his calling to love her by laying down his life. How did he do this? He had to put aside his own feelings and insecurities and figure out how she was feeling. He had to understand what she needed from him so she could grab the rope he was holding out to her and give him another chance.

The only time a soldier is weak is if he is disarmed. How do you win a woman? Instead of proving you're safe with big muscles or a sword, you prove it with sincerity. You become a man who gives his life, taking off your armor and putting your weaponry aside for her. When she comes to believe in your sincerity, she'll take off her armor as well because she knows you're not protecting yourself from her. Therefore she doesn't have to protect herself from you.

At this point, the two of you become one. As a team, you put on your armor together to protect your love from any attacks. Your wife is not your enemy—she is your love, a love worth dying for. You have to show her that you will give up your very life for her safety.

Love Offers Provision, Body and Soul

There are two ways a husband is to provide for his wife: for her body and for her soul.

Provision for the Body

Women may feel intimidated by the word *respect*, but think about your man here for a minute. We've already talked about his having to lay down his life for you. Now we will talk about his call to provide. So, as we move on, don't you think it would be appropriate to offer our men a little grace and mercy? Are you ready?

Most of the men I know have a basic understanding and drive to take care of the women they love on a physical level. In fact, many men feel inadequate if they're having a hard time making this happen.

GIVING UP TOO EASILY

Clayton recently read an article about the effects of excessive time spent playing video games. Scientists who study the brain have started to notice an interesting trend among young men. Apparently, the frequent use of video games affects the part of the brain that stimulates critical thinking. This part of the brain in gamers has become stunted, while the section of the brain that acts and reacts has become abnormally large.

What does this mean? Many young men have a shown they have a hard time taking initiative and with problem-solving. Because of this, large numbers of them have moved back home to live with their parents. They are unmotivated to find a job and provide for themselves, much less anyone else, because they give up too easily. If a job doesn't pop open, like a new level on a video game, they give up. They might apply for a few jobs, but if nothing pans out, they settle back in with Mom and Dad.

Ephesians 5:28-29 says, "Husbands ought to love their wives as their own bodies. He who loves his wife loves himself. After all, no one has ever hated his own body, but he feeds and cares for it, just as Christ does the church—for we are members of his body." First Timothy 5:8 adds, "If anyone does not provide for his relatives, and especially for his immediate family, he has denied the faith and is worse than an unbeliever."

Physical provision is expected of a husband. Why? Because this is the way God designed a man. These verses are not intended to heap condemnation on any man who is trying to provide but can't find a job or needs assistance. These verses are, however, addressing the inclination a man should have to care for his family. If you don't have a drive to do this, you need to ask yourself why, because this is the first step to understanding how to love.

Are you motivated to fulfill your duty as a husband and later as a father? If you're not currently taking care of your own obligations, how will you be able to love a woman by providing and protecting? You are not only responsible for making sure your family is provided for physically, but also with evaluating and caring for your wife's spiritual development. If you haven't found the motivation to be her physical provider, it's going to be even more challenging to fulfill the spiritual role.

Provision for the Soul

> *Husbands, go all out in your love for your wives, exactly as Christ did for the church—a love marked by giving, not getting. Christ's love makes the church whole. His words evoke her beauty. Everything he does and says is designed to bring the best out of her, dressing her in dazzling white silk, radiant with holiness. And that is how husbands ought to love their wives. They're really doing themselves a favor—since they're already one in marriage.[2]*

I love that translation! It helps us see that a man is expected to encourage and care for the soul of a woman. This role is often neglected for many reasons. Among others that could be mentioned, most men...

1. have no idea this is an expectation of a husband.

2. have no idea what this means or how to do it.

3. think this is either God's job, or the job of their wife's girlfriends, pastor, or counselor.

4. don't think they have the time or ability to give emotional support.

Ephesians 5 teaches that a man and a woman become one, just as Christ and the church have become one. The man is to provide, care for, nourish, and cherish his wife like Jesus cares for His people. I understand that this is daunting, but God will give you the strength and wisdom to do it if you are willing to work at it.

Often a man will become neglectful of a woman's emotional health and her need for loving attention because bringing home the bacon seems more urgent. In the book *For Men Only*, Jeff Feldhahn admits,

> Men focus on income and possessions because it is so much easier to measure success in numbers. "Loving attention" is much more difficult for us to quantify. Providing for our family is a commendable and biblical injunction. But we must be willing to ask ourselves whether we are delivering what our family genuinely needs, or whether we've somewhere bought into some internal or cultural assumptions that might actually be sabotaging what matters most. If so, some adjustments are probably in order. [3]

It can be confusing for a man to spend all day every day at work, only to come home to a wife who seems distant and disappointed. There are many wives and children who probably dream of having a man in their lives who is willing to work hard and steadily, so I do not want to demean this honorable pursuit. But if you truly want to love your wife, financial provision will only go so far. Consider the following comments from women:

> "Financial struggles, by definition, are difficult. But if I had to, I'd rather have them, than lose him…"

> "My husband is a very good provider, dearly loves his family, and says I complete him in every way. But he rarely seems willing to spend one-on-one time with me or to share my life, yet he always has time for the guys. I know he also needs his friends, but this lack of me in his day-to-day life is causing a big drift in our marriage." [4]

Is it possible? Right now you may be feeling like you can't win as a husband. *Work hard and provide? And now she's saying I have to give emotional support too? Not possible.*

But keep listening. Sure, it's hard to work for something that has an indefinable success point, like emotional support. You're not the only one in that boat, however. Even though you may think you aren't emotional, your wife is also intimidated to be there for you emotionally. Why? Because you *are* emotional—just in a different way than a woman.

Here is a prime example—one you will likely experience. After we had our first son, motherhood overwhelmed me. Many times I had to take care of Jacob alone, day and night, because Clayton was traveling. I was tired. Then came Joseph, and my job became even more consuming. My hands were full, and I was trying to prove myself worthy of the challenge. I wanted to perform excellently as a mom while also trying to maintain some semblance of adult interaction. (Notice the words *job* and *perform*.) I was so occupied with my duties to my kids that I didn't notice my husband's uncharacteristic withdrawal. He became distant and pensive. Occasionally, I would intend to ask if he was okay, but the crying, feeding, burping, and diapers were so consuming that the quiet thought of concern became lost in the chaos.

Finally, I suppose in desperation, Clayton shared with me that he was jealous. He said I was spending a lot more time on the kids' needs than on him, and it seemed like I was neglecting him.

What? Was he really telling me he was jealous of my time with the boys? Did he not think I would rather spend time alone with my caring husband, who was able to speak intelligible English, than with my adorably taxing children? I was completely caught off guard by his emotions. Honestly, they seemed a little ridiculous to me.

I had never intended to leave him out—I was just trying to *get the job done*. To be fair, we were both feeling underappreciated. I was overwhelmed at meeting everyone's needs and putting mine on the back burner, and Clayton was watching me care for everyone but him. I never suspected he was feeling jealous. But when he confessed, I understood. Our main issue was that we were in that infancy and toddler stage with our kids. However, we also needed to *take control* and find time for ourselves. We could meet these emotional needs if we communicated and worked in cooperation with each other. This is what love looks like.

Getting ready to care for your mate's soul. Men and women are both emotional, and often we have weaknesses that share the same space, so to speak. Clayton felt jealous of my job. What was my job? Taking care of our kids day in and day out. Was this job important? Yes. Was it necessary? Yes. But it was also necessary for us to take control or we would damage or lose our marriage in the process. I needed to help my husband in his feelings, to serve him. Just because his feelings seemed unreasonable to me didn't make them invalid.

Maybe your loved one's emotions are confusing to you, as Clayton's jealousy was to me. A person's feelings are valid *not* because *we understand them*, but because *they feel them*. So, even if their feelings don't make sense to you, they make sense to them. If we are going to build up and encourage our mate's soul and not just provide for their body, we must become a place where our mate feels safe and nurtured. They don't need solutions. They need support.

Here are some practical ways to prepare yourself to care for the soul of your mate:

1. Suspend your opinions and logic for a while so you can adequately listen to their struggle.

2. Remind yourself that their feelings are valid simply because they feel them, not because they make sense to you.

3. Don't try to explain their feelings away.

4. Remind yourself that you were probably attracted to the ways in which your spouse differs from you, and refuse to become resentful.

5. Pray for one another, and believe that the prayer of a righteous person is powerful and effective.

As Paul says, "No one ever hated his own body, but he feeds and cares for it."[5] We have to make efforts to care for one another's emotions. Loving your spouse's body and soul as your own is a change in attitude. Their needs, whether physical or emotional, are as important to you as your own. Resenting differences will divide, but attempting to understand will bring you together. Men and women most often become disconnected when they neglect each other's needs. Your spouse will find emotional support somewhere. Wouldn't you rather they find it in you than in someone else? This is why we are called to love body and soul.

Christ's goal was to present His bride radiant, without stain, wrinkle, or blemish; holy and blameless. As a man, you are obviously not capable of saving your wife's soul, but will you manage your marriage in a way that helps her find safety and strength of body and soul so she can grow in spirit? Your desire to sustain and protect your wife physically is not an excuse for emotional neglect. You could lose your job and your house, but if her soul is safe and secure in your love, she will be rich. What if you have the most successful business ever and she has every possession she could ever want, but her soul becomes bitter because she doesn't have you?

Love Offers Connection

I know all of this talk about being willing to love may seem a bit overwhelming. Do you feel incapable of loving by giving emotional support and spiritual guidance? You probably should. Does it surprise you that Jesus is calling you to something beyond yourself? Why does He always issue challenges that make us feel inadequate?

The simple truth is, you *are* inadequate to love like this on your own. And once you realize that, you can surrender and begin to trust in and rely totally on Jesus. If you only had to provide physically, you might feel able to do it yourself. However, He gives you a bigger challenge, one that forces you to depend on Him or else fail miserably. This is the essence of living in Christ and living out Christ. It's not about what we need to do, but who we need to be—children of God who depend on Him for every need.

The First Connection

The only way to give love in this way is to be connected to Christ. This excerpt from *Having a Mary Heart in a Martha World* by Joanna Weaver is helpful in encouraging us to find our strength and sustenance in Christ, the life-giving Vine:

All our "do and do," our "rules on rules," will never accomplish what Jesus can when we let him have his way in our life. But in order for that to happen we must be connected to him. It's not enough simply to be associated. To be acquainted. We have to be spiritually grafted on—to draw our life from him, to be so closely attached that we would wither and die if we were cut off...

It's the tree, not the branch, that determines the fruit. The tree is the life source. The branch has no power of its own. But once it gets connected, once that sap gets flowing and those leaves start growing, that insignificant little twig will find itself loaded with fruit. And it didn't have to do anything—except abide.

My relationship with God works the same way. My sole responsibility is keeping my connection to Jesus solid and secure...As trite as it may sound, the formula for intimacy with God remains the same today as it has always been:

PRAYER + THE WORD + TIME = INTIMACY WITH GOD.[6]

Just as this author suggests, often our Christian walk becomes more about what we're doing instead of Who we're trying to know. We replace communion with a list of tasks, rules, and rewards. We're too busy working *for* Him to receive *from* Him. Work becomes the focus, and we are left dry. We are the dry stick on the ground, trying to produce fruit with no lifeline, no nutrition to make our apple grow. If we were on the tree, we'd simply ingest the nutrients and water the tree was providing. Instead, we lie dead on the ground, trying to make our own. If we miss intimacy it's because we're missing connection.

How do prayer, the Word, and time create intimacy with Christ?

Prayer is how you express yourself to God, and He will respond by either listening or speaking back. When you pray, the relationship becomes closer because you are sharing conversation.

Taking in the Word is how you learn more about God's ways, thoughts, and character. We know that God already knows us fully, but there is so much to learn about Him, and His story is written in the Word. When you read the Word, you learn His story.

Time is needed with any relationship. Some of the time you spend will be in prayer and the Word. During this time, as with photographic film and light, you expose yourself to Him and you begin to "absorb the image of his character, his love, his wisdom, his way of dealing with life and people."[7] I also think you can spend time with Him through doing things you love. I paint with God. You may love to run or write songs or build things or create beautiful art. The point is to spend time with Him.

Applying the Intimacy Equation

Let's translate this into marriage.

First, Christ gives us the motivation and ability to love. Our second motivation is the relationship with our spouse. Your lover isn't marrying you for your services, but for your friendship. You need to be connected. So we apply the same equation—prayer, the Word, and time equal intimacy.

Prayer in marriage is time in conversation. You cannot keep up with someone if you don't communicate. Talk about your day, your plans, friends, family, frustrations, hopes, fears, and successes. Share yourself with your spouse. Don't lose touch with each other. When you come home together, turn off the TV and computer—maybe even your cell phone—and converse. It's amazing how much intimacy entertainment and distractions can steal from you if you let it happen. If you are going to be connected, you have to talk.

The Word is your story. Learn to read your spouse. Who you are now is not who you will be in 50 years. Your marriage will be an evolving story. You've had your own story for a while, who you are and what you've become. But now your story will involve someone else. Watch your mate and listen to them. Observe who they are becoming and what they are learning. Talk about your story and share it with one another. Clayton and I talk about our story with one another. We talk about who we were, who we are now, who we hope to become. We reminisce and recall what God is doing through and in us. When your stories blend together, people will look at you—even just one of you—and see both of you because your marriage tells a tale. You belong together, and people want to read the book of your romance!

Time is simply time. Spend time together. I like to paint with God. This is an activity. Find the things you love as a couple and do them. Coffee shop and dinner conversations are nice and intimate, but there is a time for fun together. Do activities you both enjoy. And if you haven't found any, work on it. I've always loved to snow ski. Clayton, not so much. But after a few good ski trips out West with good snow, he's developed a fondness too. I used to sit in a deer stand with him just because I wanted to be with him. Don't neglect having fun together. You're married, not in prison.

The key to loving is in being with one another. If you try to do the things in this book without being connected to Christ and your spouse, you will fail. You may both be working on those things, but you will miss each other. Loving is intimate and personal. If it becomes just another task, your spouse will feel abandoned.

When we avoid one another because we don't understand each other, when we tune each other out because we feel like the other person is being illogical, irrational, or emotional, we fail to connect and we fail to love.

Our mission is to get in the mire and muck of our mate's life, to listen when we don't understand, to look past offenses in order to see the person we married. Husbands, this is your lifework. Wives, this is your lifework. Love is willing to crawl on the floor and get dirty.

When we humble ourselves, we can begin loving. When we serve and listen and seek to understand, we begin to love. When we protect and provide, we are loving.

This is love. This is Christ. This is marriage. Are you willing to do this?

Chapter 12

Are You Ready
to "Get Naked"?

Whe Charie and I were writing this chapter, we knew it
would be the first one the guys would turn to. We know the
title is a bit provocative. But the fact remains that in a healthy
marriage, you will have to "get naked" in front of each other. Both
physically and emotionally.

I'd like to go on record and say that I really enjoy the sexual intimacy
my wife and I share. Plainly put, sex is fun. But that is not all it is, and
if you go into marriage thinking that sex will be uncomplicated, that
you can get it anytime you want it, or that it's as easy as cooking dinner or flipping on a movie, then you will be severely disappointed and
tragically surprised. So let's be as honest as we can here.

We may say some things that make you feel embarrassed or
uncomfortable (nothing crass or off-color, of course), but we are willing
to do that. We'd rather you deal with the issue now in spite of the awk-
wardness than waltz into marriage clueless about the complexities of sex.

So: We are going to talk about sex. We are going to be bold and
biblical. We are doing this because we are delighted with this gift from
God and want the best for you as you too enjoy it. If you're grown-up
enough to consider marriage, then you're grown-up enough to have a
frank conversation about sexuality.

Caught Off Guard

The worst thing that can happen to you in this area is to enter into marriage unprepared mentally and emotionally. Sex is a big deal. It can be one of the tenderest expressions of love and trust, or it can be used as a means to manipulate and enslave one another. You don't want to get caught clueless!

In this life, there's little that is more embarrassing that being caught in, well, a certain position physically. Charie and I were "in bed" one morning. We had the door locked to make sure our boys didn't wander in like kids are known to do. Thinking we had taken every precaution to ensure the safety of our intimacy, all of a sudden we heard the door pop open. We froze, peered toward the door through the dark, and saw our two-year-old son standing in the doorway with a screwdriver in his hand. He had picked the lock. Praise God he was only two and the room was dark! Even though we thought we knew what we were doing, we were caught completely off guard (and it ruined the moment). So, just because you think you understand how sex works is no guarantee you won't be caught off guard.

This is the great challenge in our culture. Because America is so sex-saturated and because people are so open about sex in the media, we think we know all about it. In reality, we know nothing about it as a culture—because if we did, we wouldn't be so flippant about something that is so delicate, powerful, and sacred.

TEN BASIC POINTS

Here are some basic observations about sex that both husband and wife need to be aware of before they get married.

- Sexual experience does not make you an expert. It doesn't even mean you're good at it or that you know what you're doing. In fact, it may be an obstacle to overcome.

- You will spend less than 1 percent of your married

life having sex. The other 99 percent is where trust, intimacy, and communication are established.

- Honeymoon sex is awesome. Enjoy it while you can. The rest of your marriage will not be like the honeymoon.

- Sex with your spouse won't be anything like the movies make it out to be. Don't expect tears, a soundtrack, and choirs of angels.

- Just because you're married doesn't mean you get sex anytime you want it. (All the married people just shouted *amen.*)

- Sex does not begin when you take your clothes off, and sex does not end when you put your clothes on.

- The environment you create in your home creates or destroys opportunities for meaningful, intimate lovemaking.

- The level of intimacy you create in conversation will be equivalent to the level of intimacy you experience when you make love.

- A word to the guys: A clean house is the same thing as foreplay. Helping your wife with chores is an aphrodisiac.

- A word to the girls: Taking off any item of clothing is foreplay. A smile, a nod, a wink, basically just walking in front of him, is foreplay.

For Men Only

Helpful Insights from Clayton

As a man, I can testify that prior to marriage, sex was the one thing

I most looked forward to. By God's grace, I remained a virgin until my wedding night, as did Charie. One of the things that gave me strength to resist temptation was the anticipation of being able to finally "get naked" with my wife on our honeymoon night and go all the way. I was terrifically excited to be able to give her the gift of my purity, and I had created a vision in my mind of what sex would be like once we tied the knot.

It was everything I had hoped for and more. But I soon began to see that sexual intimacy was much, much more than a physical act. It was emotional, spiritual, and conversational.

So as you prepare yourself for marriage, don't assume that the bedroom will just take care of itself. Sex is a very different experience for the man and the woman early on in the relationship, and I'd like to share some insights with you that will help you understand your wife emotionally and sexually before your "first time" together.

The "turn on" switch. Just like a room has a switch you flip to turn on the light, men and women have sexual switches. They are totally different, and you need to be aware of this.

Guys are visual. We enjoy things that look good, and to us, there is nothing that could ever look better than a woman. This is how God wired our brains. Consequently, the more skin a woman shows, the more our eyes are attracted to her. She doesn't have to say or do anything to catch our eye. She just has to be a woman.

This initial phase of attraction is usually what hooks us. We are not thinking about her intellect, her personality, her dreams and hopes for the future. We are simply stunned by her appearance—and if we like what we see, we take the next step.

Unfortunately, even after marriage some guys never get beyond this step. We are content to provide for our family and make sure our wife has all the things she needs, and we hope to have sex as often as possible. If you become this stereotypical husband, your wife will starve emotionally. Why? Because sex is how men get their emotional needs met, but sex is not the way women feel loved, admired, and appreciated.

Women are more emotionally complex. A woman's "turn on" switch is intimacy. And by that I mean she must feel cherished, understood, protected, and cared for. The way she feels all these things is through being close to her man. She will not feel close to you unless the two of you *talk*.

Open up! The way to prepare yourself to "get naked" sexually with your wife is to get honest with her and open up. The magic word is *conversation*. This is hands-down the biggest turn-on for women. They love to talk, but they really *need* to talk with their husbands. You, the man, hold the keys to sexual intimacy and pleasure. So the sooner you learn to talk to her about your feelings, your fears, and your burdens, the closer she will feel to you, and in return, the happier and more fulfilled you will both be in the bedroom.

You need to make yourself talk. It won't come naturally to you. You will have to work at it. Let her help you.

Listen aggressively. One of the greatest needs in a woman's heart is to be understood. It is also fairly simple for the man to learn how to do this, because for the woman, if you are listening to her, you are understanding her (even if what she is saying makes no sense to your male brain at all).

1. When she is talking, turn off all things with a switch: computers, cell phones, televisions, music, and so on. She needs your undivided attention without any noise or distractions.

2. Make eye contact the entire time she is talking. Don't look away. Affirm her with smiles, nods, and moans and groans, and say things like, "Wow, I had no idea you felt that way. Please tell me more!"

3. Don't share your confusion with her while she's talking. You need to be listening. Let her talk, and remember that she processes her feelings differently than you do. She doesn't just want to talk about one big thing that she is excited about or bothered about. She wants to talk about everything! And for her, talking *is* processing.

4. Affirm her as she talks and let her know that even if you don't totally get where she's coming from, you love her and are willing to listen and learn and offer support.

Clean the house. You may think this has nothing to do with sex. But it has everything to do with sex, because for the woman, intimacy and trust precede sex. And there is no better way to get close to your wife than to prove to her you want to help out with little things she feels she has to do.

Your wife will feel overwhelmed with chores, laundry, meals, dishes, errands, possibly work, and later on, kids, so when you offer to help out, not only are you building a friendship with her by serving her, but you are taking things off her to-do list, which means she will more likely want "to do" some other things in the bedroom with you later.

Clean yourself. Here's where the advice gets down and dirty: Learn good hygiene!

Women like things to be clean and well ordered. After you've helped scrub toilets and fold clothes and clean the floors…after you've worked outside…after you've done whatever…take some time to spruce yourself up. Cut your fingernails and toenails. If she likes a smooth face, then shave. Shower and put on something that smells good. Charie and I have a deal where I agree to wear anything she buys for me, including clothes and cologne. So if she likes the way a cologne smells, I wear it. Duh! You can fix up without turning in your man card.

Give gifts. This is not brain surgery, guys. Women love to get gifts from their man, and it's not so much about the present or how much it costs. When you give your wife something, even something small, it communicates to her that you were thinking about her when you were away from her, and this assures her of your love for her. Get in the habit of bringing small things home, and she will begin to look forward to seeing you walk in the door. Find out what she likes and get it. Then get creative and surprise her with a scarf, a handbag, a pair of shoes or boots, earrings, her favorite candy, flowers, a card, or a handwritten letter.

Ask early. We guys only need about nine seconds of lead time to be ready for action, but your woman needs way more time than that. Don't wait until you're brushing your teeth before bed to ask her for sex! Ask her early in the morning if you can make love that night, or ask her before you go to bed if you can make love the next morning. This gives her plenty of time to think about it and prepare herself, and the more she thinks about it, the more she will want it, and the better it will be for both of you.

Don't take it personally. If you ask for sex and get turned down, she is not rejecting you. It has nothing to do with your desirability. She may be exhausted, stressed, worried, or overwhelmed about work or family issues. She may be emotional from her period or may be feeling unattractive because she thinks she's put on a few pounds. If she communicates that she doesn't feel like sex, assure her that you love her and that it's okay. Nine times out of ten, you will take the pressure off her by saying that. And before you know it, she is waking you up in the middle of the night for some "special time."

Lead her spiritually. Because sex is so spiritual, it's important that you lead your wife as the two of you pursue knowing Christ. Pray *with her* and pray *for her*. Hold her hand when you pray. Pray over her at night while lying in bed. Read Scripture with her. Sit beside her at church with your Bible and notebook. Share with her the things God is showing you in your devotional life—and by all means, be weak enough to open up to her about your doubts, fears, and struggles. She will relate to you on a more intimate level when she knows she is not the only one in the marriage who doesn't have it all figured out spiritually.

Date her. It is paramount that you do fun things together. Go to nice restaurants. Take walks. Go to the movies. Have a date night each week. Take vacations. Steal away for an evening at a hotel or to a bed-and-breakfast in another town. Remember how you chased her when you were dating? Well, you don't break up when you get married. Just because you caught her doesn't mean you stop pursuing her.

When I am feeling sexually frustrated, all I have to do is *look at myself* and ask some questions. Keep this list handy after you get married.

1. Am I gently leading her spiritually?
2. Am I too busy with work or projects to notice her?
3. Have we been on a date recently?
4. Is the house a wreck? Am I serving her by helping out in the home?
5. Are there unfinished things on my "honey do" list?
6. Have we sat and talked for more than five minutes in a while?
7. Has she seen my eyes linger on another woman recently?
8. Am I giving her "advance notice" so she can prepare for sex?
9. Am I being kind, verbally affirming, and encouraging with my words, my tone, and my body language?
10. Am I being thoughtful with gifts and the little things I know she appreciates?

Your woman is continually giving you a steady stream of information about who she is, how she feels, and what she needs. If you will become a student of your wife, paying attention to her and studying her, you will figure out the best way to love her. The more secure and the closer to you she feels, the better your sex life will be.

Remember, men—you set the tone. She responds to you. If you want to *make love*, you have to *give love* first.

Place me like a seal over your heart, like a seal on your arm; for love is as strong as death, its jealousy unyielding as the grave. It burns like blazing fire, like a mighty flame. Many waters cannot quench love; rivers cannot wash it away. If one were to give all the wealth of his house for love, it would be utterly scorned.[1]

—THE SONG OF SONGS, CHAPTER 8

For Women Only

Helpful Insights from Charie

I am truly excited to write this chapter with Clayton because the gift of physical intimacy in marriage is so wonderfully fulfilling and mysterious. Animals can mate, but only humans make an emotional and spiritual connection during sex.

Many people have a hard time combining spirituality with sexuality (so they probably avoid the Song of Songs!). If they are disconnected in your thinking, I pray you will change your opinion as you get ready to "get naked" physically and emotionally with your husband in marriage.

Women, know this: You will be the only legitimate source of sexual pleasure your husband will ever have. That should make you feel secure, not afraid. For the rest of your life, your husband will desire you, your love, and your friendship. (And your body, and yes, sex. Lots of sex.)

Revealing Love

Clayton and I went to a secluded cabin for our honeymoon, and we shared a lot of intimacy! I woke up the third morning thinking, *What have I done? Does God still love me?* I was having a little bit of an identity crisis because everything had changed overnight. One day, I'm a virgin who dresses modestly, and the next day, I've had sex and am free of all restraint. I needed some assurance that this was okay. You will probably go through something similar.

I asked Clayton if he shared my conflict. He looked completely confused and said, "No way, this is awesome!" He was clueless. But so was I, and you will be too. It's okay!

Boy, have I come a long way since then! I've learned a few things about my man (and men in general).

Your man is way more visual than you. What does this mean? He notices you now, but when you get married, he will want to look at you even more. He will enjoy staring at you when you're getting dressed, when you take a shower or a bath, when you're putting on lotion, when getting ready in your robe in the bathroom.

I don't know how you will react to this. You may be embarrassed, you may feel offended, or you may love it and play it up. Your past will dictate your reaction to your husband's natural desire for you. But you need to be prepared, because it's not a bad thing (it would be bad if he never looked at you at all!). This is how God made him. Accept it and be thankful that he wants you. My husband often asks me, "Aren't you glad that I find you attractive? Wouldn't it be awful if I didn't think you were the most beautiful woman alive?" This is a great question, because it *would* be terrible! I *want* him to think I'm beautiful and sexy. Your husband will think you are the hottest thing since lava. He will prove it by looking at you, touching you, pursuing you, and asking you for sex.

If you read the Song of Songs, the Lover, Solomon, is constantly complimenting his wife. He admires her tan cheeks, tall neck enhanced by long earrings, lovely face, round peaceful eyes, classic nose, long shiny hair, white teeth, sweet and luscious lips, tongue of milk and honey, beautiful feet, graceful legs, good figure, and playful breasts. When we read about his affections, it may seem a little embarrassing, but we know in our hearts it shouldn't be any other way. Learn to love the fact that your man finds you irresistible!

Giving Permission

When you get married, you need to give him permission to enjoy you. When he compliments you, receive it instead of deflecting it. If he admires you, say thank you and learn how to soak it in. Be "visually generous." Not only will he love touching your body, he will love looking at your body. It's his nature, so enjoy the attention he gives you, and remember that it's his way of expressing his love for you.

Why should you enjoy your husband's admiration of your body? A few reasons. First, it's very difficult to know how to react to a person who is never able to receive compliments. If you really don't know how to take his comments, talk about it and figure out why. Are you insecure about your appearance, like the Shulamite woman in the Song of Songs? She asked Solomon not to stare at her because she had been "darkened by the sun."[2] Apparently her family had made her work long hours in the garden and her dark skin wasn't attractive to her. She mentioned this to him, and he complimented her all the more. She gained confidence in Solomon's view of her. She realized she was his standard of beauty. He is constantly saying she is beautiful, the "most beautiful of all women," and he rejoices, "All beautiful are you, my darling; there is no flaw in you." He also adds, "My dove, my perfect one, is unique."[3]

The Shulamite embraced the fact that she was everything her husband desired in a woman. Why is this important to grasp? Because this idea will set the stage for an amazing sex life for the two of you. You can enjoy each other without wondering if you need to be more than you are. The Shulamite comes to really believe that she possesses his heart, because her husband says, "You have stolen my heart, my sister, my bride; you have stolen my heart with one glance of your eyes with one jewel of your necklace."[4] She confesses, "My lover is mine and I am his." She is convinced he is looking at no one else, and this gives her confidence.

I was insecure when Clayton and I first married, and even more after children, because I compared myself to everyone around me. When Clayton would compliment a certain feature of mine, I would shrug it off, and a dozen pictures would flow through my mind of women with a better "fill in the blank." I was too busy comparing myself to see myself through his eyes. He wanted me, wanted to look at me and enjoy me. I wouldn't let him fully do this because I didn't think I measured up.

We have to be okay with being the standard for our men. When we let them enjoy us, they find satisfaction and pleasure. This does not mean you are an object. Many women have suffered abuse, and so this is the perspective from which they view their husband's desire for them. You will not be a toy or an object but a wife, and this means you're the one woman in the world who has the ability to satisfy your husband. Now he's yours to have for your satisfaction, and you're his to hold on to as well. Your body used to belong to you alone, but now you get to share it with the one man in the world you think is worthy of your life and love.

When we were first married, I would cover up with something pretty before we made love, then shortly afterward put something else back on. And I wanted everything to take place with the lights off. Clayton never complained, but through his tenaciously admiring my body I started to see myself as he did—and now I'm not afraid of the light anymore! After we enjoy each other, I'm not running for cover. We can lie together and talk uninhibited, unashamed like Adam and Eve, as God intended, and it's wonderful. Prepare yourself to work toward losing your inhibitions. The longer you're together, the easier it will get.

Welcome to Wonderland

To your man, your body is a wonderland. A popular song by John Mayer recently celebrated this very thing. (I'm not sure the characters in the song were married, but the truth remains.)

This leads me to my next point. God wants you to enjoy each other, and enjoy each other often. The Song of Songs speaks of the lovers inviting each other into sexual relations. The Lover takes his time to get his Beloved ready for love in 7:1-7, and then he can't wait. He says, "I will climb the palm tree; I will take hold of its fruit. May your breasts be like the clusters of the vine, the fragrance of your breath like apples and your mouth like the best wine." After looking at her and admiring her, he wants to be with her, to touch and enjoy her body. And what is his Beloved's response? "May the wine go straight to my lover, flowing gently over lips and teeth. I belong to my lover, and his desire is for me. Come, my lover…"[5]

You may be blushing, but that's good! I'm here to tell you that God wants you to delight in your mate. Sexual intimacy between a man and a woman is God's gift of fun and entertainment in marriage. He wants us to have fun and enjoy each other. The bedroom is a playground! Your husband will want to experiment, so embrace his childlike exuberance over being naked with you.

And remember that for your man, his greatest feelings of intimacy with you come when you are making love. That is his refuge, his place of safety and security and trust. Sex for him is not just intercourse. It's you! You are his paradise.

Fearing Love

A majority of women experience fear and intimidation when they think about sex in marriage. If you feel unprepared, awkward, or uncomfortable during your engagement, find a godly married woman you trust and ask her to spill the beans about everything that is concerning you! Ask her also if you can pour out what's weighing on your heart. More women are entering marriage with the baggage of abuse, rape, or a list of sexual regrets from previous relationships, so don't allow the shame of your past to cripple you before you walk the aisle.

Don't assume that if you're "experienced" before marriage that this makes you an expert with your husband. The opposite may be true. "The natural joy of sexual awakening is ruined by premature experimentation. Maximum sex is marital sex. The best sex is believer's sex."[6] If your experience was not within marriage, you need to learn from a godly married woman. You may also need the help of a wise, experienced counselor. It's better to let someone help you than to settle for a mediocre sex life. God will honor your desire for wholeness and healing.

Realistically, making love is not like what happens in the movies. They have the perfect music, mood lighting, and film editors. Movies are not real, but you are real, so you may need to adjust your expectations. I find that when you take sex too seriously and try to make everything perfect, your expectations are never met, and you don't receive pleasure as a woman (it's hard to have an orgasm when you're not relaxed). Talk with your husband about what you enjoy and what relaxes you. Communication is a major part of good lovemaking. Talk a lot. Laugh a lot. Play and have fun! If you can't have a good time and get goofy in the bedroom with your husband, then where can you?

Plan to have sex a day in advance so you think about it all day long. Make playful suggestive comments to each other. Seduce your husband. Play games. Be silly. Get creative. Don't always wait on him to make the advances. Your man will love it when you take charge in the bedroom! Come up with your own secret phrases and inside jokes. Sometimes we ask each other, "Would you like an apple tonight?" making reference to the apple tree in the Song of Songs: "Like an apple tree among the trees of the forest is my lover among the young men."[7]

So let yourself go! He is your husband! He'll be your biggest fan, and the more you please him in the bedroom, the more he will please you in every area of your marriage. Are you ready?

Final Considerations

Here is some compelling data to encourage you before you get married.

A Barna Update reported that "the goals that most adults identify as their top priorities in life are healthy living, possessing a high level of integrity, and keeping one marriage partner for life."[1]

A review of more than 130 studies on the relationship between well-being and marital status [concluded] that married people have significantly lower rates of alcoholism, suicide, psychiatric care, and higher rates of self-reported happiness…a lower rate of severe depression than people in any other category…Married women were about thirty-three percent more likely than unmarried women to rate their emotional health as "excellent"…Nine out of ten men married at forty-eight will still be alive at sixty-five, while only six out of ten single men will be.[2]

The marital commitment is not only healthy for the body, but also has a positive effect on the emotions and the soul.

But what about sex? Does it get boring in marriage? If you cohabit, you leave your options open and can test the waters, right? Consider these statistics:

Married sex beats all else...Married women had much higher rates of usually or always having orgasms, 75 percent, as compared to women who were never married or cohabitating, 62 percent. And, the researchers wrote, "Those having the most sex and enjoying it the most are the married people."[3]

On the other hand,

We now know "physical and emotional satisfaction start to decline when people have had more than one sexual partner"..."Cohabiting couples compared to married couples have less healthy relationships...Cohabitants experienced significantly more difficulty in [subsequent] marriages with [issues of] adultery, alcohol, drugs and independence than couples who had not cohabited." In fact, marriages preceded by cohabitation are fifty to one hundred percent more likely to break up than those marriages not preceded by cohabitation..."Aggression is at least twice as common among cohabitants as it is among married partners."[4]

Again, God's design is proved healthier than unfounded ideas and opinions. He wanted His children to experience sex at its best, joined together and discovering love's delight for all their years on earth.

God also knows that marriage is healthier for the entire family.

Children who grow up in a household with only one biological parent are worse off, on average, than children who grow up with both of their biological parents, regardless of the parents' race or educational background...because it often leaves them in the care of highly stressed and irritable mothers...Children without fathers often have lowered academic performance, more cognitive and intellectual deficits, increased adjustment problems and higher risks for psychosexual development problems...

The report also notes that many children of divorce become dysfunctional adults. They have more failed romantic relationships, a greater number of sexual partners, are two to three times as apt to cohabit, are less trusting of fiancés, less giving to them, and twice as likely to divorce. When both are from divorced homes, their risk of divorce is as much as 620 percent higher in the early years of marriage. Thus the "marital instability of one generation is passed on to the next."[5]

Maybe you are one of these children. Join the club. Clayton's mother abandoned him, but God gave him a wonderful family who protected and loved him. I am a child of divorce—my mom and dad have both been married three times. But when Clayton and I consider these statistics, we applaud the God we serve—because He changed our statistics.

So, we'd like to encourage you. Your future doesn't have to be determined by your past. We know God has done this for us, and we have faith He can and wants to do it for you.

Our desire is to provide hope in a world that has turned its back on marriage. If following God's statutes has worked for us, it will work for you.

> *How can those who are young keep their way pure? By living according to your word. I seek you with all my heart; do not let me stray from your commands.*[6]

Again we see that God's design for marriage and sex proves to be smarter and healthier than all other ideas and opinions. And why not? He created them.

✷

Marriage is a wonderful thing. Now that you have asked the questions, are you ready?

Notes

Chapter 5—Will You Tell the Truth?

1. Romans 6:19-23.
2. Lewis Smedes, *The Art of Forgiving* (New York: Ballantine Books, 1997), 20.
3. Gary Thomas, *Sacred Marriage* (Grand Rapids, MI: Zondervan), 89
4. Darlene Harbour Unrue, *Katherine Anne Porter: The Life of an Artist* (Jackson, MS: University Press of Mississippi, 2005), 42.
5. Thomas, 70.
6. Jennifer Rothschild, *Me, Myself and Lies* (Nashville, TN: Lifeway Christian Resources), 13, emphasis added by author.
7. Smedes, 21.
8. Smedes, 177-178.
9. Oswald Chambers, *Daily Reflections with Oswald Chambers*, December 7, 2010, www.freerepublic.com/focus/f-religion/2638701/posts.
10. 1 John 4:16-18.
11. Smedes, 21.
12. Thomas, 34.

Chapter 6—Will You Commit?

1. Gary Thomas, *Sacred Marriage* (Grand Rapids, MI: Zondervan), 15.
2. Ruth 1:8-9.
3. Ruth 1:16-17.
4. Daniel Block, "Ruth," *The New American Commentary*, vol. 6, ed. Kenneth Matthews and David Dockery (Nashville, TN: Holman Reference, 1999), 605.
5. Thomas, 31.
6. Proverbs 1:10 TNIV.
7. Psalm 1:1-3 TNIV.
8. 2 Corinthians 10:4-5.
9. Thomas, 26.

Chapter 10—Are You Willing to Submit?

1. NLT.
2. Ephesians 5:21-25,28,33.
3. Craig Keener, *Paul, Women, and Wives* (Grand Rapids, MI: Baker Academic, 1992), 160.

4. Keener, *Paul*,161.

5. Keener, *Paul*,164.

6. Keener, *Paul*,166-167.

7. Ephesians 5:1-2.

8. Ephesians 5:2 NLT.

9. Carolyn Custis James, *Lost Women of the Bible* (Grand Rapids, MI: Zondervan, 2005), 35.

10. 1 Peter 2:21-23.

11. 1 Peter 3:1-4,7.

12. Craig Keener, *The IVP Bible Background Commentary: New Testament* (Downers Grove, IL: IVP Academic, 1994). 717.

Chapter 11—Will You Give Respect?

1. Francine Rivers, *Redeeming Love* (Colorado Springs, CO: Waterbrook Multnomah, 2007), 460-461.

2. Shaunti Feldhahn, *For Women Only* (Colorado Springs, CO: Waterbrook Multnomah, 2004), 22-23.

3. Linda Dillow, *Satisfy My Thirsty Soul* (Colorado Springs, CO: NavPress, 2007), 119.

4. Feldhahn, 182.

5. Ephesians 2:10 NLT.

6. Adapted from Psalm 39:14.

7. Adapted from Ephesians 2:10 NLT.

8. Gary and Betsy Ricucci, *Love That Lasts: When Marriage Meets Grace* (Wheaton, IL: Crossway Books, 2006), 70.

9. Nicholas D. Kristof and Sheryl WuDunn, *Half the Sky: Turning Oppression into Opportunity for Women Worldwide* (New York: Vintage, 2010), xv, xvi, xvii.

10. Psalm 44:21.

11. Lewis Smedes, *The Art of Forgiving* (New York: Ballantine Books, 1997), 6-7.

12. www.quotesaboutlife.ca/author.html?a=Johann+Wolfgang+von+Goethe.

13. Paraphrased from Colossians 3:12-19.

14. Andreas Köstenberger, *God, Marriage and Family*, 2nd ed. (Wheaton, IL: Crossway Books, 2010), 15-16.

15. Proverbs 16:3.

16. Gary Smalley, *Loving Each Other for Better and for Best* (Nashville, TN: Nelson, 2005), 237.

Chapter 12—Are You Ready to Love?

1. Francine Rivers, *Redeeming Love* (Colorado Springs, CO: Waterbrook Multnomah, 2007), 308.

2. Ephesians 5:25-28 MSG.

3. Shaunti and Jeff Feldhahn, *For Men Only* (Colorado Springs, CO: Waterbrook Multnomah, 2006), 92, 95.

4. Cited in Feldhahn, 86, 89.

5. Ephesians 5:29.

6. Joanna Weaver, *Having a Mary Heart in a Martha World* (Colorado Springs, CO: Waterbrook Press, 2000), 79.

7. Weaver, 76-77.

Chapter 13—Are You Ready to "Get Naked"?

1. The Song of Songs 8:6-7.

2. The Song of Songs 1:6.

3. The Song of Songs 1:8; 4:7; 6:9.

4. The Song of Songs 4:9.

5. The Song of Songs 7:9-10.

6. Daniel Akin, *God on Sex: The Creator's Ideas about Love, Intimacy, and Marriage* (Nashville, TN: B&H Books, 2003), 52.

7. The Song of Songs 2:3.

Final Considerations

1. Daniel Akin, *God on Sex: The Creator's Ideas about Love, Intimacy, and Marriage* (Nashville, TN: B&H Books, 2003), 104.

2. Akin, 97-98.

3. Akin, 97.

4. Akin, 97.

5. Akin, 99-101.

6. Psalm 119:9-10 TNIV.

A Word from Clayton About Crossroads Worldwide...

In 1995, I began a nonprofit ministry out of my college dorm room called Crossroads.

It began with my preaching ministry and now includes multiple layers of ministry that stretch all around the world.

- *Summer camps.* Several thousand middle- and high-school students come from all over the United States every summer to our Crossroads summer camps, where they hear teaching and preaching from God's Word and participate in group activities, sports tournaments, corporate worship, and community missions.

- *Student conferences.* Every January during Martin Luther King Jr. weekend, we host a three-day conference for middle- and high-school students, as well as a separate conference for college students and young adults.

- *Mission trips.* We send short-term volunteer teams to India, Malaysia, Haiti, the Navajo reservation in Arizona, and various other places to share the gospel. We also support a full-time volunteer couple in the Himalayas as they assist in running a Christian hospital.

- *Community discipleship home.* We host two intensive discipleship programs for people ages 18 to 25, one in Boiling Springs, North Carolina (a 12-month program) and one in Manali, North India (a 6-month program).

- *Preaching ministry.* I travel full-time, teaching and preaching on evangelism, discipleship, missions, and relationships. I speak at conferences, colleges, churches, retreats, concerts, and public schools. I began this ministry at age 14 and have preached in 45 states and 30 countries to over 2 million people.

- *Writing.* In addition to the five books I have written, I consistently write about issues that face Christians, pastors, leaders, parents, and spouses on my blog at www.claytonking.com.

- *Media.* I have dozens of audio and video sermons online for free. Find them at

www.claytonking.com
www.newspring.cc
www.liberty.edu
iTunes: "clayton king live" or "clayton king"

For more information or to schedule
one of our speakers, contact us at

www.crossroadsworldwide.com
crossroadsworldwide@gmail.com
704-434-2920

More from Clayton

was adopted when I was just a few weeks old and raised in a Christian home, learning the values of hard work, simplicity, respect, and honesty. I always dreamed of making a career out of football, but God had other plans for me.

I converted to faith in Christ at age 14 and began preaching the gospel in prisons and local youth groups in the eighth grade. Since then I've preached to over 2 million people in 45 states and 30 countries. Besides serving as president of Crossroads Worldwide Ministries (see above), I serve as teaching pastor at Newspring Church in Anderson, South Carolina, as well as campus pastor at Liberty University. I've also authored several books, including *Dying to Live* and *Amazing Encounters with God.*

I'm a graduate of Gardner-Webb University in North Carolina, and I've been married to Charie since 1999. We have two sons, Jacob and Joseph. I love to spend time with my family, read good books, eat good food, drink good coffee, and be with good friends.

A Word from Charie

I was born and grew up in Atlanta, Georgia, but when I attended Appalachian University in North Carolina, the attractions of the city began to wane compared to the delights of nature. I decided to pursue an education in recreation management and began leading trips rock climbing, caving, rafting, and camping.

God first used my desire for missions when He led me to Mexico in high school. In college I traveled to Romania and Poland. With Clayton, I have traveled to India, Israel, and many places in the U.S.

First and foremost, however, I am a wife and mom. My husband and I are committed to put our relationships with the Lord, each other, and our family before our duties to "ministry," for if we lose each other, we lose the most precious assets the Lord has given us.

I have always enjoyed finding truth in the treasure of God's Word, as well as a calling to divide it properly and teach others. So, I am thankful for the doors God has opened for me to speak at Crossroads Worldwide events and women's events, and also to travel and teach alongside my husband.

Writing and artwork: Several years ago I wrote a book entitled *Behind the Veil: A Journey Toward Grace.* I hope to revise and expand that book sometime, as well as write another with my husband sometime soon, but until then you can always read my online blog, which is on my website. There you can also see some of my oil paintings. I simply want to glorify God with what I paint, and use it for good. As long as I like it, I'm pleased. So, if you are interested, you can take a look at my works online. I hope they minister to you. *www.charieking.com.*

Other Harvest House Books by Clayton King

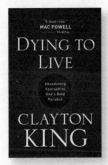

Dying to Live
Abandoning Yourself to God's Bold Paradox

Do you want to *live*? Do want to be sold out to something that will outlive you and outlast your existence? Then you have to die. It's the only way to gain life. The only way to fill that deep-inside longing. The only way to really know Christ—because it's *His* way.

Clayton King shares 20 bold pictures from Scripture, his own life, and the lives of others that will

- make you sick of existing just to get more stuff, money, and "success"
- grip your soul with longing for the life Jesus promised
- stir up your passion for God's mission to build a kingdom that will last forever

It's a reality that's no longer about you.

> *"You wake up to a world filled with colors and tastes and textures and conversation and songs and laughter, a world that no longer revolves around your own petty drama but around God's bigger story of rebuilding what we have all broken."*

Amazing Encounters with God
Stories to Open Your Eyes to His Power
CLAYTON KING

Where do you want to meet God today?

Author Clayton King points to real-life experiences that show how God speaks through the everyday occurrences of life. At any moment, He is there, giving you the chance to open your eyes to Him—as happens when Clayton…

- has an enlightening conversation with a drunken millionaire on an airplane
- witnesses a miracle of biblical proportions in a small Himalayan village
- plans what he thinks will be a quick down-and-back hike to the bottom of the Grand Canyon
- considers a horse sticking its head through a barbed-wire fence
- has a surprise encounter with the IRS

These compelling, thought-provoking stories will encourage you that God is always at work in your life, even in the very ordinary. And when He breaks in with the unexpected—which happens about a trillion times a day in our world—you can step back, pause for a moment, and gaze in awe and admiration.

More Resources to Help You with Relationships

Sex, Food, and God
Breaking Free from Temptations, Compulsions, and Addictions
DAVID ECKMAN

The good things created by God, like food and sex, can be misused to run away from emotional/relational pain. When this happens, the damage and loneliness can wreck your life.

David Eckman shows how and why unhealthy appetites trap people in a fantasy world, and how shame and guilt—and the addiction cycle—are broken when we realize how much God delights in us.

101 Questions to Ask Before You Get Engaged
H. NORMAN WRIGHT

How can I be sure?
Is he really right for me?
Is she the one?

Deciding to spend the rest of your life with someone is one of the biggest decisions you'll ever make. The key to a successful marriage is getting to know your partner *before* you make the plunge. Relationship expert and noted couples counselor Norm Wright will steer you through a series of soul-searching questions—even difficult ones that need to be addressed—to help you discern if you've met "the one."

Before You Say "I Do"™ DVD
H. NORMAN WRIGHT

In this video, bestselling author and marriage counselor Norm Wright draws from his many interactions with couples to help you discover more about your and your future mate's dreams and goals for your marriage. You'll learn enduring principles for lifelong partnership as you begin to

- adjust to differences in personality and background
- clarify role expectations
- develop your spiritual life
- establish a positive sexual relationship
- talk over how to handle finances

Most of all, as you discover the role that Jesus Christ has in your relationship, you and your partner will gain what you need to make your marriage all it's meant to be.

Based on the million-selling Before You Say "I Do"™, *the go-to resource for premarital counseling, and presented by the author*

Dating with Pure Passion
More than Rules, More than Courtship, More than a Formula
ROB EAGAR

There's more to true love than you've been told. Rob Eagar shares the forgotten, Christ-centered answer to the relationship issues you face. *Dating with Pure Passion* is the path to...

- recognize God working on your behalf

- break the cycle of fruitless relationships

- find and attract healthy singles

- appreciate sexual desire and resist temptation

- handle the pressures to get married

> "*Dating with Pure Passion* is a great resource for anyone seeking God's design in lasting relationships."
>
> LOUIE GIGLIO
> Founder of Passion Conferences

Includes a Bible study and discussion guide for personal use and for small-group studies.